T0001324

The Green Witch's Guide to Self-Care

The GREEN WITCH'S Guide to SELF-CARE

Natural Spells, Rituals, and Remedies for Your Mind, Body, and Spirit

Autumn Willow

ROCKRIDGE PRESS

No book, including this one, can ever replace the diagnostic expertise and medical advice of a physician in providing information about your health. The information contained herein is not intended to replace medical advice. You should consult with your doctor before using the information in this or any health-related book.

Copyright © 2022 by Rockridge Press

All rights reserved. No part of this publication may be reproduced, stored in a retrieval system, or transmitted in any form or by any means, electronic, mechanical, photocopying, recording, scanning, or otherwise without the prior written permission of the Publisher. Requests to the Publisher for permission should be addressed to the Permissions Department, Rockridge Press, 1955 Broadway, Suite 400, Oakland, CA 94612.

First Rockridge Press trade paperback edition 2022

Rockridge Press and the Rockridge Press logo are trademarks or registered trademarks of Callisto Media Inc. and/or its affiliates in the United States and other countries and may not be used without written permission.

For general information on our other products and services, please contact our Customer Care Department within the United States at (866) 744-2665, or outside the United States at (510) 253-0500.

Paperback ISBN: 979-8-88608-093-3 | eBook ISBN: 979-8-88650-476-7

Manufactured in the United States of America

Interior and Cover Designer: Stephanie Mautone
Art Producer: Sue Bischofberger
Editor: Alexis Sattler
Production Editor: Ellina Litmanovich
Production Manager: Riley Hoffman

Illustrations © Travis Stewart

10 9 8 7 6 5 4 3 2 1

*To the game
that saved my life.
For the Horde!*

CONTENTS

INTRODUCTION

WELCOME AND CONGRATULATIONS ON TAKING THE FIRST STEP TOWARD HEALING AND SELF-CARE. I am Willow, a modern-day hedge witch, teacher, and novice herbalist. With almost twenty years of magical experience, I've learned how to use my craft to sustain my mundane (or nonmagical) life, promote my own healing, and practice self-care. I am also a teacher, and in addition to helping me create a sustainable work-life balance, witchcraft has allowed me to find joy and peace in a difficult profession. Witchcraft can do the same for you, as well as help you heal past traumas, reduce stress, and promote overall wellness.

I started practicing witchcraft when I was in high school. I was fortunate enough to be raised by two supportive, open-minded parents who let me do my thing, even though they were cautious of my desire to practice. I appreciate them for this, as it has opened the door to so many possibilities, connections, and spiritual growth spurts I wouldn't have experienced otherwise. What my friends found indoors at church, I found outdoors in nature. My practice has gone through many changes over the years, and I finally settled into hedge-craft, which combines green witchcraft with spirit communication and exploration of the connection between the physical and spiritual world. I am absolutely obsessed with plant folklore and love finding new ways to integrate my practice into healing and self-care. Isn't that what spirituality is supposed to be: a guide to living your best life?

I wrote this book because I feel now, more than ever, that it's needed. Witchcraft is an act of resistance and radical self-care. In a society that promotes rugged individualism, protects corporations over people, and systemically oppresses large portions of our population, witchcraft is a way to fight back. However, you can't fight back if you aren't taking care of yourself and your community first. I have used green witchcraft to help me sleep better, fight off the flu, turn my home into a sanctuary, protect my neighborhood from terrible storms, and even fight against an oppressive government. These acts of self-care ensure I can continue fighting for the highest good. Exploring green witchcraft will help expand and enhance your self-care practice as well.

Though the activities are centered around green witchcraft, this book is for everyone, no matter your faith, income, or experience level. Self-care and healing are attainable for everyone, not just those bound to a specific path or lifestyle. It's my sincere hope that you will take something away from this book that helps you on your journey. Witchcraft has transformed my life for the better, and I hope that it will do the same for you.

It's time to take control of your destiny. Let's get started, shall we?

How to Use This Book

This book is divided into two parts. Part 1 is a basic introduction to green witchcraft, its origins and role in healing and self-care, and the correspondences and tools used. You will also find brief guides on how to live sustainably, decolonize your self-care practice, and even set up your own garden. This introduction is not comprehensive, and I encourage you to supplement these chapters with the resources listed at the end of the book. Witchcraft requires continuous learning, so know your journey doesn't end here. Part 2 contains fifty-five natural remedies, rituals, and spells for healing and self-care that you can incorporate into your daily life. They are organized alphabetically by ailment and include healing methods for your mind, body, spirit, home, and community.

You can interact with this book in whatever way you please. Read it from start to finish or flip to a specific spell or remedy depending on your needs. However, reading through part 1 first will lay the groundwork for a successful practice. I encourage you to experiment with witchcraft whenever you can. As with anything else, the remedies, rituals, and spells will come more easily over time, so take the time to experiment and learn. Remember to have patience with yourself as you become more comfortable putting what you are learning into practice. It takes time to develop a good rhythm that works for you.

I

PART I

The Power of Green Witchcraft for Self-Care

This part includes three short chapters that explore the power of green witchcraft and how it can be used in your self-care routine. Chapter 1 dives into the practice of green witchcraft, its origins, and benefits. You will also learn how to live sustainably and harness the power of the natural world. Chapter 2 describes how to use green witchcraft as a pathway toward healing and self-care. It also explores what self-care is and is not, the benefits of self-care, and how to decolonize your self-care practice. Finally, chapter 3 offers a brief overview of the tools used in green witchcraft, including the magical properties of different candles, crystals, essential oils, and plants. You will learn how to set up an altar, keep track of your spell work, and prepare for rituals. These chapters will lay a foundation for the practices described in part 2.

Chapter 1

Unveiling the Way of the Green Witch

reen witchcraft is among the fastest-growing branches of witchcraft. Many people are searching for paths outside traditional religion and modern capitalism, looking for something free, sustainable, and wild. In this chapter, we unveil the way of the green witch. We will explore what green witchcraft is and is not, spanning from its humble beginnings to modern practices. You will learn how to honor the earth and harness the power of the natural world. We will also explore how nature impacts modern life, and how, when used alongside medical advice and best practices, nature can help reduce the symptoms of mental illness or lower the risk of cardiovascular disease. Green witchcraft provides us the opportunity to rewild our lives, live more sustainably, develop our intuition, and reveal insights and lessons about ourselves. Come along as we journey through time and explore the magic of green witchcraft.

What Is Green Witchcraft?

Green witchcraft is a secular, earth-based practice that combines the use of natural objects, folk magic, and sustainable, environmentally friendly rituals to honor the earth and nature spirits. Green witches are often naturalists, healers, and environmentalists who seek to use the earth's wisdom and resources to enact positive change. In today's human-centered society, green witchcraft emphasizes and celebrates our interconnectedness with nature. It opposes the trend toward disconnect, which has resulted in the exploitation of not only nature but also humans, leaving many feeling overtired, overworked, and undervalued. Green witchcraft provides the opportunity to change this.

Green witchcraft shares many commonalities with kitchen witchcraft and hedge witchcraft, such as the use of cooking, folk magic, and natural objects, but green witchcraft centers its practice on the earth and our connection to it. The green witch views natural places as sacred and works to reduce their footprint by living sustainably. Furthermore, green witchcraft is not a religion and therefore has no central dogma like that found in Wicca. Green witches may or may not incorporate deities into their practice, celebrate holidays, or subscribe to the Wiccan Rule of Three, as practiced by many Wiccans.

The Origins of Green Witchcraft

Green witchcraft is a relatively modern invention, but humans have always had someone in their communities in charge of healing, magic, and so on. We even see this in some prehuman hominids ritualistically burying their dead. There is evidence of people practicing midwifery as early as 40,000 BCE—the Paleolithic era. Many practices that are used in green witchcraft date back to the work of midwives and cunning folk, the naturalists, herbalists, and healers who provided an invaluable service to their towns. These individuals lived in harmony with nature and knew how to use the earth's natural bounty to their advantage.

Unfortunately, many of these practices slowly died away due to industrialization, as large groups of people moved into the cities and away from the countryside in search of work. In subsequent decades, modern medicine overshadowed folk medicine, dismissing folk magic as "baseless superstition."

It wasn't until the 1960s and 1970s that we began to see a resurgence of occult, nature-based practices, such as Wicca and neo-druidism, which just so happened to correspond with the rise of the hippie counterculture movement. This radical movement rejected the mores of mainstream American life and religion, instead centering communal living, environmentalism, inclusion, and peace. As a result, Wicca and other nature-based practices grew in popularity, eventually giving rise to modern green witchcraft, which offered a more inclusive, sustainable, and welcoming alternative to traditional religion and spirituality.

The Role of the Green Witch Today

Modern green witches still identify with the historic titles of healer, herbalist, and naturalist, as well as more modern titles such as environmentalist. Green witches may center sustainable practices of their ancestors like land management and conservation, while also incorporating more modern practices like recycling and renewable energy, all with a dash of magic. Some green witches rely heavily on local folk magic, but others embrace globalism, incorporating practices from around the world while being mindful of appropriation.

With the increasing threat of climate change, the rise of late-stage capitalism, and a desire to connect with our ancestors, more and more people are turning away from traditional religion in search of something different, something *more*, to fill the void many of us feel. Humans have an innate desire to belong to a community and embrace a wildness that's difficult to find in cities. Green witchcraft offers an alternative to mainstream spirituality, and its nature-centered focus has resulted in a gradual rise in interest over the last thirty years. Modern green witchcraft is largely solitary, but it still maintains a strong focus on the importance of family and community.

The Impact of Nature in Our Modern Lives

Historically, our ancient ancestors spent the majority of their lives outside, living off the land. Our ancestors were plagued by hardships we no longer suffer, but they also reaped the benefits of living so close to nature. Advances in technology and medicine have decreased infant mortality and increased our average life span, but our disconnect from nature has led to what journalist Richard Louv calls "nature-deficit disorder." Symptoms include "diminished use of the senses, attention difficulties, and higher rates of physical and emotional illnesses." The further we move away from nature, the more we suffer and the less we desire to protect it.

If you are looking to prioritize healing and self-care, the first step is recognizing the healing powers of the natural world. Studies have shown that being in nature reduces stress and cortisol levels, lowers heart rates, and alleviates symptoms of anxiety and depression. Access to common green spaces also reduces the impact of air pollution and noise pollution. Furthermore, the earth offers a variety of natural remedies and magical tools the modern green witch can use to their healing advantage.

The Benefits of Green Witchcraft

For centuries, witches were regarded as healers, midwives, and cunning folk who could cure everything from a headache to a heartache. These witches understood the value of stopping and slowing down, of listening instead of speaking. They learned the healing ways of the earth and used them to create remedies, both magical and mundane. They transformed their communities and their lives for the better. By following the path of the green witch, you, too, can experience the same benefits as our witchy ancestors. Through green witchcraft, you will strengthen your connection to the natural world, discover hidden truths about yourself, live consciously, and develop your intuition.

Green Witchcraft and Sustainability

Sustainability is a key tenet of environmentalism; it's the meeting of our needs while preserving resources for future generations. The green witch incorporates sustainability into their daily practice to protect the earth and ensure there is plenty for generations of green witches to come. This act of preservation is both practical and spiritual. Green witches are often animists: people who believe that everything, both living and nonliving, has a spirit or energy. Because of this, all of nature becomes sacred, and the act of caring for the earth becomes an act of devotion. This improves a green witch's magical ability, enhances magical creativity, and builds mutual trust between the witch and the spirits they work with.

However, sustainable acts need not be expensive. The green witch uses natural resources close to home. Whether they live in cities or near large green spaces, in their magical practice they make use of anything from the dandelion poking through a cement crack to a dropped feather of a local bird, taking no more than what they need. They reduce, reuse, and recycle where possible, recognizing the magic even in the most mundane of items. Jars are reused as spell bottles and for storage; old clothing is turned into poppets and sachets. The modern green witch is resourceful, just like the witches before them.

Strengthen Your Connection to the Natural World

Green witchcraft provides you with the perfect opportunity to strengthen your connection to the natural world. Green witchcraft centers Mother Earth, recognizing that the earth and all living and non-living things possess a spirit and vibrate with energy. Green witches hone their craft by connecting with these spirits, learning the magical and medicinal properties of natural objects, and living by the rhythmic cycle of nature.

Through this connection, the green witch embraces the teachings Mother Earth has to offer. The green witch embraces the inevitability of change, the never-ending cycle of life and death, and the inter-connectivity of all of life. Connecting more deeply with the natural world results in magical benefits, such as plant allies that assist you in your practice, but it also provides numerous health benefits, such as lowering stress.

Encourage Self-Discovery

Practicing green witchcraft also encourages self-discovery. One of the biggest lessons the earth teaches us is how to listen. Often, we listen with the intent of responding. Through quieting our minds and connecting with the grounding energy of the earth, we open ourselves up to hearing our inner monologue. This allows us to reflect on who we are, which areas of our life need attention, and where our past traumas lie so we may heal.

The earth also teaches us the value of perseverance. From the dandelion reclaiming the sidewalk to recovering populations of mountain gorillas, life finds a way. Discovering that you, too, are capable of persevering allows you to overcome obstacles. It is through self-discovery that real, lasting changes are made.

Live Consciously

Because green witches seek to live in harmony with the earth, they are acutely aware of their impact on our planet and how to reduce their harm. That isn't to say that green witches never engage in environmentally unfriendly activities. None of us, even the most privileged, are capable of reducing our ecological footprint to zero. But we can be conscious about how our actions directly impact more than just ourselves. As such, green witches are mindful of the products they purchase, the companies they support, and the resources they waste. The green witch knows when to and when not to take, and how to thank the land spirits and earth for the gifts they provide.

Develop Your Intuition

As with all forms of witchcraft, green witchcraft helps develop your deep inner knowing—intuition. Intuition bridges the gap between our conscious and unconscious mind, thus surpassing our five senses. When harnessed correctly, intuition can improve just about every aspect of your life. Connecting more deeply with your intuition can strengthen your relationships, help you achieve your goals, and empower your magic. Most important, developing our intuition allows us to move toward authentic growth and contentment. When you cast a spell, you work with energies within yourself to bring about your intention, making magic a naturally intuitive experience.

Honor Your Relationship with the Earth

Above all else, green witchcraft will help you honor, explore, and strengthen your inherent connection to the natural world, a connection our ancestors understood well. In such spaces, it's important to extend that honor and respect to the practices of indigenous populations in the workings of their craft. Green witches recognize the innate value of preserving nature, finding the sacred even in the mundane. With an animistic perspective, green witches recognize that all nature is sacred and deserving of respect and protection. For example, the spirits of land are known as genius loci, and many magical rituals are built around honoring the land with routine offerings.

Green witchcraft promotes natural exploration and encourages you to be observant of even the tiniest of creatures. Enhance your practice by spending time outdoors, learning your region's local wildlife, wildcrafting, gardening, and listening to spirits around you. Green witches often develop relationships with spiritual allies, especially plants and animals, through meditation and energy exchange. This process involves reaching out intuitively to such spirits to communicate with them and bonds the green witch with their surroundings. The earth is the ultimate healer, and green witchcraft will aid you in harnessing such healing energies.

Harness the Power of the Natural World

Everything in the natural world vibrates with energy or spirit, and this energy can be harnessed for spell and ritual work. Plants can be turned into herbal remedies, nourishing meals, soothing teas, powerful wands, fragrant incense, and ritual offerings. Stones, especially those you find locally instead of purchasing, can be used to help you ground, center, and connect with the healing energies of the earth. As you deepen your connection to Mother Earth, you learn how to incorporate the power of these items into your daily life.

In addition to using the bounty of the earth, green witchcraft also offers an opportunity to connect with and harness the power of the moon, sun, and stars. The moon causes the ebb and flow of the tides; the sun bathes the earth with nourishing rays; the stars teach us to navigate even in the darkest of times. In learning more about these relationships, you will gradually become aware of the cycles of the earth, learn to live in harmony with nature, and become comfortable using the earth's powers to enhance your everyday life.

Key Takeaways

In this chapter, we unveiled the way of the green witch. We explored how the practice has grown and changed over time, the benefits of practicing green witchcraft, and how we can use the power of the natural world to help us heal.

- Green witchcraft is a secular, earth-based practice that combines the use of natural objects, folk magic, and sustainable rituals to honor the earth and nature spirits.

- Modern green witches identify as healers, herbalists, and naturalists who center sustainable practices and magic.

- Being in nature reduces stress, lowers heart rates, and alleviates symptoms of anxiety and depression.

- Green witchcraft will help you strengthen your connection to the natural world, discover hidden truths about yourself, live consciously, and develop your intuition.

- Green witchcraft allows you to harness the power of the natural world.

Chapter 2

Green Witchcraft as a Pathway to Self-Care

elf-care is the latest buzzword among self-help influencers, life coaches, and lifestyle witches, but what is it really? In this chapter, we will explore the meaning of self-care and how it is interconnected with green witchcraft. We will take a look at how self-care goes beyond the individual and how healing ourselves can help our communities heal as well. Self-care is about filling our cups and our cauldrons. You will learn the benefits of self-care and healing, the role of green witchcraft in self-care, and how to decolonize your self-care practice so it feels inclusive and welcoming for everyone. We will also discuss the roles of time and patience in your healing journey and highlight the five areas of focus for healing and self-care: mind, body, spirit, home, and community.

Defining Self-Care

The World Health Organization defines *self-care* as "the ability of individuals, families, and communities to promote health, prevent disease, maintain health, and to cope with illness and disability." When we hear the phrase *self-care*, many of us think of solo activities or even selfishness. Self-care, however, is not just about filling your cup (self), it's about filling your cauldron (community).

The mainstream promoters of the modern self-care movement are largely cisgender white women (which I am), and the general focus of their content is solely only on the individual. Often, this focus leaves community- and family-oriented cultures out, as if self-care is not an integral part of community care. This couldn't be further from the truth.

In this book, you will find a nature-based, community-centered approach to self-care and healing. Self-care is the bridge to community care and healing. As we heal each other, we can better heal ourselves, and vice versa. Green witchcraft is the perfect companion to self-care and healing because Mother Earth and her bounty offer a myriad of health benefits. With that being said, healing and self-care through magic and spell work can and should complement other healing modalities, including therapy and modern medicine; you don't have to choose one or the other.

The Benefits of Exploring Self-Care

Healing and self-care are essential to living a long, healthy life. Studies have shown that routine self-care reduces and even eliminates anxiety and depression, improves concentration, promotes happiness, reduces stress, and improves energy—the same benefits associated with nature. Furthermore, healing and self-care are acts of liberation and resistance. Capitalism is a relatively new invention that encourages productivity and maximum efficiency; self-care teaches us the opposite. When we center ourselves and communities, instead of corporations and productivity, we fight systems of oppression. The short-term goals of healing and self-care center the individual, and the long-term goals include healing communities. With these practices, you will learn to prioritize your needs, deepen your self-knowledge, reduce the effects of anxiety and depression, and even break cycles of ancestral trauma.

Prioritize Your Needs

Socrates, when asked to sum up his philosophical commandments, stated, "Know yourself." Caring for ourselves is an act of self-love and community service. When you engage in self-care, you learn to put your own needs first. This allows you to recharge and refocus, allowing you to better serve your community.

Self-care and healing are all about prioritizing your needs, which can be difficult for the empathetic green witch. In general, witches tend to be very in tune with the energy around them, and therefore often prioritize others over themselves. From an early age, we are taught the virtue of selflessness as something we should all strive for. But being too selfless can cause major damage. Putting yourself on the back burner and hoping someone else will fill your cup will leave you emotionally, mentally, and physically drained.

Deepen Your Self-Knowledge

Healing and self-care require self-reflection. Through journaling, meditation, and shadow work, you deepen your self-knowledge, which gives you the power to influence your future. When combined with witchcraft, self-care becomes a powerful tool for creating positive change.

Knowing yourself makes you a better decision-maker and improves communication skills, self-confidence, and self-regulation. When you commit to understanding yourself more fully, you expand your ability to empathize and understand the perspectives of others. Furthermore, deepening your self-knowledge helps you pinpoint past traumas and the behaviors associated with those traumas. Without self-reflection, self-care is like putting a small bandage over a serious injury; eventually, you are eventually going to need something stronger. By pursuing self-knowledge, you can find holes in your cup and mend them from within.

Reduce the Effects of Anxiety and Depression

Roughly 18 percent of adults in the United States have anxiety disorders, and 7 percent have major depressive disorder. Self-care can help alleviate the symptoms associated with these mental illnesses by alleviating stress, creating endorphins, and generating a relaxing environment. However, there is a danger when you approach self-care as something you *should be* doing. When self-care becomes just another thing on the to-do list, it is normal to feel guilty when you cannot complete the task. This guilt then exacerbates symptoms of depression and anxiety. In order to reap the benefits, you must recognize that your self-care will not look like anyone else's. It's not about perfection, and it doesn't have to be a stress-inducing task. If self-care is approached in a healthy way, it can be used to manage anxiety and depression in conjunction with medical assistance.

Break the Cycle of Ancestral Trauma

Ancestral trauma, also called intergenerational trauma, is trauma that passes between generations. According to epigenetic inheritance theory, environmental factors can manifest genetically as a chemical tag that latches to our DNA and switches genes on and off. This trauma is commonly caused by enslavement, genocide, forced relocation, destruction of cultural practices, famine, and other cataclysmic events such as a pandemic. Symptoms include alcoholism, depression, drug misuse, numbness, and withdrawal. Self-care can help you break the cycle of ancestral trauma through healing, reflection, and self-discovery. You can learn how to set boundaries, reconnect with your cultural roots, recognize negative self-talk, and process feelings regarding your family system. These skills will aid you in becoming a cycle-breaker and gift you with a new family legacy.

Enhance Your Healing Journey with Green Witchcraft

Because green witchcraft centers nature and Mother Earth, it pairs well with self-care and healing. Green witches attempt to live in harmony with the natural world as much as possible, thus reducing stress, increasing happiness and focus, and promoting overall wellness, which is necessary for healing and self-care. Green witchcraft also provides a unique opportunity to expose yourself to new ingredients and tools outside the norm of traditional self-care. You can enact lasting change by learning about both the magical and medicinal properties of natural tools. Green witchcraft also makes space for creativity and experimentation, as there are no set rules for practicing. In that way, green witchcraft inherently provides an outlet from the rigid structure of our capitalist society. Finally, green witchcraft helps reveal the power within and around you, highlighting your strength and value outside of your presumed productivity.

Exposure to New Ingredients and Tools

By incorporating green witchcraft into your self-care practice, you expose yourself to a wide variety of ingredients and tools that are not common in the mainstream self-care movement. Green witchcraft uses the magical and medicinal properties of local plants for herbal remedies and powerful healing magic, allowing you to incorporate these powerful allies into your daily life. Learn about techniques such as dendrotherapy, earthing, and forest bathing. By tuning in to the natural cycles of the earth, you learn how to eat and live seasonally, which aids in healing and overall health. Finally, green witchcraft exposes you to the healing properties of natural objects like crystals and running water, along with the benefits of natural processes such as breath work.

Space for Creativity and Experimentation

Because there are no set rules, green witchcraft makes space for creativity and experimentation. What works for one witch may or may not work for another, which forces us to try new things and experiment magically. The spells in part 2 should be used as guidelines, not doctrine. Lean into your local ecosystems and spirits for magical support. Change the ingredients, wording, and movements to better suit your needs. If a spell fails miserably, recognize this failure as an opportunity to learn and grow. The experimental nature of green witchcraft necessarily results in creativity and acts as an outlet from modern-day expectations. Being creative is just one of the many steps you can take on your self-care journey.

Reveal the Power Within and Around You

The practice of working with your unconscious mind to uncover repressed or hidden behaviors, emotions, and thoughts is called shadow work. Like all types of witchcraft, green witchcraft incorporates energy work and self-reflection through shadow work. This practice can help you reveal and harness energy so that you may direct it toward practical, lasting change. Our capitalist system is rigged to leave individuals feeling energy-depleted and powerless, but witchcraft has historically been used by marginalized groups to fight against their oppressors. Take back your personal power and use it to defy systems of oppression to heal yourself and your community. Witchcraft, like self-care and radical healing, is an act of rebellion. Revealing the power within you provides you with an advantage. Use it.

Live in Harmony with the Natural World

Practicing green witchcraft teaches us to live in harmony with the natural world. Green witches respect Mother Earth, follow the cycles of the earth and moon, and work with the spirits of the land. Living in harmony with the natural world has a ripple effect. One study reported participants felt less entitled and self-important after looking up into eucalyptus trees for one minute, and that watching just five minutes of the *Planet Earth* docuseries caused people to view their worries as insignificant. Living in harmony with nature helps us put our lives into perspective and gives us a sense of meaning and interconnectedness. Nature is a powerful teacher.

Embrace Healing and Self-Care Through Green Witchcraft

Green witches address healing and self-care through remedies, rituals, and spells that focus on the mind, body, spirit, home, and community. When you dig into part 2, you will find fifty-five spells that address these five tenets in a wide variety of ways, ensuring that everyone is able to partake. Some spells involve cooking a nourishing meal, and others bind the actions of those who wish to do harm. Remember, self-care is an act of resistance.

Magic can aid you in your journey, but it should not be the only tool you employ. Keep in mind that each of the spells and rituals found in part 2 require you to take mundane action as well, such as going to therapy, supporting your community and participating in activism, volunteering your time, or financially supporting humanitarian and environmental charities. Combined, you will create a sustainable healing and self-care practice you can share with your community.

Mind

In part 2, you will find remedies, rituals, and spells that focus on mental and emotional health and wellness. The mind encompasses your mental self—where creativity, emotions, imagination, intellect,

Decolonizing Your Self-Care Practice

As with most pop culture fads, the modern self-care movement is entrenched in colonialism and generally represents a superficial, consumerist approach to healing. Many of the practices we often associate with self-care originated from cultures that had their practices violently stripped from them and commercialized. Employing a debased version of these culturally significant practices, the mainstream self-care movement actively excludes marginalized groups through the correlation of self-care with whiteness, femininity, and wealth. However, you can take steps to decolonize your self-care practice to include everyone.

◆ Avoid practices that appropriate from a culture that you are not a part of. For many, that includes chakras, smudging, sweat lodges, and yoga. If you wish to take part in one of these practices, join a group led by people who are part of the culture from which it originated, pay accordingly, and treat the experience with respect.

◆ Understand that self-care is for everyone and looks different for different communities. All self-care methods are valid. If you are white, decenter whiteness and create space for marginalized groups.

◆ Rest, and rest often. Your worth is not determined by your productivity.

◆ Take a holistic approach to self-care by focusing on mind, body, and spirit. Goal-centered perfectionism is counterintuitive to self-love.

◆ Incorporate ancestral practices and honor your ancestors. Connecting with your roots will help you heal ancestral trauma and create a self-care practice that works for you.

and thoughts manifest. The mind is therefore paramount to healing and self-care, because mental health overflows into all aspects of life. Without healing the mind, you cannot work on healing your physical and spiritual self, let alone others in your home or community. An unwell mind often manifests physically as fatigue, muscle soreness, and even illness. Furthermore, the mind is where your magic begins. It's where you initially express the need for change, formulate the words and actions, and direct energy. Without it, your magic will get nowhere fast.

Body

Your body is composed of all the complex systems that allow you to move, breathe, and exist in this corporeal realm. It is your spirit's anchor to the physical world. Your physical health has a direct impact on your mental and spiritual health, and therefore cannot be left out of self-care. In fact, imbalances in the mind or spirit are often not noticed until they manifest physically. Unlike other approaches, however, you will find this book focuses on healing your body from within, practicing mindful relaxation, and developing a routine of low-impact movements to strengthen your body without focusing on weight loss or fitness.

Spirit

Rounding out our pyramid of self-care is the act of tending to our spirit. Your spirit is your energetic self, the part of you that seeks meaning and purpose. Nurturing your spirit can help you find clarity, fulfillment, and peace so you can live a happier, healthier life. Witchcraft plays a key role in spiritual health, as it provides a means to understand our higher self and the unexplainable world. Witchcraft also provides an opportunity to exert some control over our lives when we otherwise feel powerless. In part 2, you will find remedies, rituals, and spells to help you find balance and peace and develop your intuition. You will also learn how to enlist spirit guides to aid you in your self-care journey.

Home

In order to fully embrace healing and self-care, you must create a happy, safe, and secure environment that nurtures growth and allows you to practice your craft. For some, this may be incredibly difficult to achieve, as your home may not be safe and secure for various reasons. Maybe you are not free to practice openly for fear of retaliation or you live with an abusive parent, partner, or spouse. Regardless of your situation, it's important to find a space that *is* happy, safe, and secure. In part 2, you will find a series of inconspicuous methods to create a magical wellness sanctuary, even if it's just a bathroom shower, bedroom closet, or hidden alcove in a local park.

Community

When we heal ourselves, we heal our communities. Trauma, which can arise from experiences such as abuse, racial injustice, and sexual violence, isolates the survivor. Many trauma victims feel separated from the healing energies of their communities. Colonization stripped many cultures of their community- and family-oriented practices, leaving many of us feeling utterly alone and broken. When we heal ourselves, our trauma doesn't disappear. Instead, it becomes manageable and loses its isolating power over us. Self-care also provides the opportunity to heal generational trauma, fight systems of oppression, and conserve our environment. In part 2, you will find spells and rituals that address healing your community, from strengthening friendships to fighting social injustices. We fill our cups so we may fill our cauldrons.

Healing Takes Time and Patience

Time and patience are key to healing and self-care. Self-care is not a one-and-done thing; you have to work on it and develop a routine for it to be effective. As you begin this journey toward wellness, remember to keep an open mind as you explore new healing and self-care techniques and tools through spell work. Like any new practice, you will become more comfortable with the ingredients, tools, and spells of the green witch over time. If you have been practicing witchcraft for a while, integrating craft into self-care will come naturally. If you are new to witchcraft, you may find some of the practices weird. Let yourself set aside those doubts and feelings of judgment so your transformation can occur. Your healing and self-care are worth your time and effort. This book is designed to meet the needs of a diverse audience, so there is sure to be something beneficial for you buried in its pages. I encourage you to take a chance on yourself.

Key Takeaways

Building a fulfilling self-care practice means healing your mind, body, spirit, home, and community. In this chapter, we defined self-care, discussed its benefits, and learned how green witchcraft can enhance our healing journey. By prioritizing your needs, deepening your self-knowledge, and breaking the cycle of ancestral trauma, you will reap the benefits of self-care. Finally, we discussed the inter-connectedness of body, community, mind, and spirit in healing and wellness.

◆ Healing and self-care are not just about filling our cups; they're about filling our cauldrons.

◆ Self-care improves energy, promotes happiness, and reduces anxiety and depression.

◆ Green witchcraft will encourage you to explore new ingredients and tools, make space for creativity, and reveal the power within yourself.

◆ You can decolonize your self-care practice by avoiding appropriated practices, resting, investing in community care, and incorporating ancestral practices and values.

◆ Self-care and healing take time and patience.

Chapter 3

The Magical Tools of a Green Witch

In this chapter, we will explore magical tools and ingredients commonly used by the green witch, including candles, crystals and stones, incense, and plants. Many of these tools can be sourced locally or purchased from the grocery store. We will also explore how to ethically source your ingredients, follow the Wheel of the Year, and use the seasons, moon, weather, and elements to enhance your magical and healing practice. The chapter concludes with practical advice for creating a home garden, setting up your own altar, and keeping a record of your spells and rituals, and tells you how to ground, center, cleanse, and consecrate before spell work.

Gather and Respect Your Ingredients

As with all paths of witchcraft, green witchcraft incorporates magical ingredients and tools to enhance spell work and promote spiritual growth. The majority of these tools are natural and often gathered locally or made using locally sourced ingredients. These items include candles, crystals and stones, essential oils, incense, and plants. However, no tools are strictly required to practice green witchcraft, and the best ingredients and tools are the ones tailored to you and your needs.

As a green witch, the last thing you want to do is disrespect Mother Earth or the spirit of the object you are using. That's why it is incredibly important to be mindful of how and where you accumulate ingredients. When gathering items locally, ask their permission before taking them, and leave behind an offering as thanks. Treat the items with reverence and respect and honor the spirit within. When purchasing items, if you are able, try to shop small, and support companies that sustainably source their items. Be mindful of appropriation and avoid disrespecting other cultures.

After completing a spell or a ritual, you may have leftovers. How you dispose of these remnants is just as important as how you gathered the materials to begin with. Avoid disposing of environmentally unfriendly ingredients such as salt and plastic in the ground or near local water sources, and compost natural ingredients when possible.

Candles and Incense

Candles and incense are effective tools that bring fire and air into your green witchcraft practice. Fire is the element of new beginnings, renewal, change, and passion. Candles can be used to bring these properties into your healing and self-care practice to aid in your transformation. Color magic is also often employed when using candles, allowing them to function in a variety of ways.

Incense, on the other hand, represents air, the element of communication, wisdom, and intelligence. It can be used to carry messages, clear energy, promote relaxation, and enhance your focus. Here are ten commonly used candles and five commonly used types of incense and their magical correspondences:

CANDLES

BLACK CANDLE: Banishing and protection

BLUE CANDLE: Balance, peace, and truth

BROWN CANDLE: Balance, grounding, neutrality, trust, and understanding

GREEN CANDLE: Abundance, luck, and money

ORANGE CANDLE: Connection, creativity, friendship, and health

PINK CANDLE: Intimacy, love, and romance

PURPLE CANDLE: Dreams, psychic awareness, and spirituality

RED CANDLE: Energy, love, lust, and passion

YELLOW CANDLE: Creativity, focus, and joy

WHITE CANDLE: Cleansing, new beginnings, and purification

INCENSE

CINNAMON: Luck, love, money, and purification

FRANKINCENSE: Confidence, growth, and prosperity

MYRRH: Banishment, calm, curse breaking, and protection

ROSEMARY: Banishment, memory, and protection

SANDALWOOD: Healing and purification; used as an ancestral offering

Crystals and Stones

Using crystals and stones is a great way to connect to the earth's natural healing and grounding energies. A variety of crystals can be purchased from local metaphysical shops, but the best ones are often those you find. Found stones often contain multiple elements and therefore can be used for a variety of magical purposes. Listen to the spirit or energy of the stone to determine its potential uses. Unfortunately, the crystal market is largely unregulated and therefore many are unsustainably sourced or unethically mined. Always research where your crystals are coming from. Below are ten commonly used crystals and stones and their magical correspondences.

AMETHYST: Balance, divination, and psychic dreams; dispels anxiety, stress, and fear

BLACK TOURMALINE: Grounding and protection; dispels feelings of unworthiness

CITRINE: Happiness, optimism, positivity, and solar energy

CLEAR QUARTZ: Balance and power; wards off negativity

HEMATITE: Balance, detoxification, grounding, and logic; counteracts confusion

KYANITE: Communication, compassion, and peace; enhances intuition

LABRADORITE: Energizing, healing, and protection; uncovers unconscious beliefs; great for shadow work

RHODONITE: Confidence, growth, healing, love, and self-esteem; eases feelings of loneliness and betrayal

ROSE QUARTZ: Beauty, love, peace, and romance; heals matters of the heart

TIGER'S EYE: Courage, grounding, luck, self-confidence, and strength; dispels fears and anxiety

Essential Oils

Essential oils are concentrated essences of plants. As a result, they pack a powerful magical punch that can be used to dress candles, enhance spells and rituals, and promote health and wellness. Because they are so concentrated, essential oils must be diluted with a carrier oil before using externally, and if you wish to ingest them, be sure to purchase high-quality food-grade oils. Many essential oils are toxic to pets, including citrus, clove, lavender, and tea tree, so always research before using. When in doubt, avoid diffusing any essential oils if you have pets. Diffuser blends can be safely replaced with simmer pots in most cases. Below are ten commonly used essential oils and their magical correspondences.

BERGAMOT: Attracts money and success; uplifting

CEDAR: Prosperity, protection, and purification

CINNAMON: Happiness, prosperity, protection, self-love, and strength

EUCALYPTUS: Balance, calm, concentration, healing, and purification

FRANKINCENSE: Inner truth, intuition, psychic ability, and purification

GRAPEFRUIT: Balance, healing, love, and mental clarity; uplifting

JASMINE: Calm, love, and prosperity; soothes anxiety and promotes restful sleep

LAVENDER: Calm, love, devotion, grace, and serenity

PEPPERMINT: Love, mental clarity, prosperity, protection, and regeneration

SWEET ORANGE: Empowerment, happiness, inspiration, and strength; uplifting

Flowers

The green witch often uses flowers in spells and rituals. Flowers are naturally uplifting, so they are especially useful in rituals related to healing and self-care. They can be turned into incense, remedies, or teas, or used in spell jars and sachets to enhance your magical intention. They are easy to grow in gardens and pots and can be purchased at your local grocery store. Many can also be found dried in the tea section of your local grocery store. If you plan to consume any flowers, purchase food-grade herbs from a reputable source. And consult with a physician or other professional about correct amounts; some may be dangerous if taken in excess. Below are ten commonly used flowers and their magical correspondences.

CALENDULA: Dreams, happiness, healing, and psychic ability; reduces fever and soothes muscle spasms

CHAMOMILE: Money, passion, and relaxation; reduces inflammation and promotes sleep

DANDELION: Dreams, exorcism, luck, purification, and solar energy; diuretic; soothes stomach upset

HIBISCUS: Divination, love, and lust; increases circulation

HONEYSUCKLE: Generosity, happiness, luck, money, psychic visions, and sweetness

JASMINE: Dreams, love, lunar energy, prosperity, and spirituality; mild sedative and aphrodisiac

LAVENDER: Dreams, happiness, healing, and tranquility; reduces stress and anxiety

LILAC: Banishment, good fortune, protection, and support

POPPY: Fertility, prosperity, sleep, and tranquility

ROSE: Gratitude, joy, love, and romance

Herbs and Tea Leaves

Herbs and tea leaves are probably the most used plant material in any witchcraft practice, especially green witchcraft. They are used to create candle dressings, herbal remedies, incense, magical teas, spell sachets, and so much more. They are among the most versatile of ingredients and many can be found in local green spaces and grocery stores. If you plan to ingest any wildcrafted herbs, ensure they were not sprayed with herbicides or other chemicals. Do not ingest or burn herbs picked in heavily trafficked areas, as they could contain high levels of contaminants. And be sure to consult a physician or other professional about safe amounts for consumption. Below are ten commonly used herbs and tea leaves and their magical correspondences.

BASIL: Love, luck, prosperity, and protection; fights inflammation

BLACK TEA: Courage, luck, stability, and strength; boosts energy and alertness

GREEN TEA: Health, longevity, love, and passion; improves brain function

MINT: Luck and protection; wards off bad dreams, evil spirits, and negative energy; heals muscle soreness

MUGWORT: Astral travel, dreams, and psychic abilities

ROSEMARY: Alertness, memory, and wisdom; improves brain function

RUE: Banishing, justice, and protection

SAGE: Abundance, cleansing, and purification; reduces bloating, gas, and stomach pain

THYME: Courage, happiness, health, and protection; wards off nightmares; antimicrobial

YARROW: Health and wellness; antimicrobial, reduces fever and gastrointestinal discomfort

Trees and Houseplants

Trees and other plants, including houseplants, are wonderful plant allies. A plant ally is a plant you have a close spiritual relationship with, like a friend helping you in your magical practice. The green witch can use plant allies in their magical healing and self-care practice, as well as general witchery. Trees can be used to create charms, healing remedies, incense, and wands. Houseplants can be used in much the same way as trees, but more often, they are used to change the energies in a home by offering protection, purifying energies, and promoting happiness. When working with any type of plant, be respectful of its spirit. Ask for permission before harvesting pieces and be sure to leave offerings as thanks. Below is a list of ten commonly used trees and houseplants and their magical correspondences.

AFRICAN VIOLET: Love and support

BIRCH: Beauty, purification, renewal, and strength; pain reliever

HAWTHORN: Death, health, love, marriage, and protection; improves circulation and lowers blood pressure

JADE PLANT: Abundance, energy, and wisdom

MAPLE: Balance, longevity, protection, and tolerance

OAK: Abundance, fertility, luck, protection, and strength

PALM: Protection, safety, and solar energy

POTHOS: Forgiveness, protection, and resilience; helps purify the air and eliminate odors

SNAKE PLANT: Purifying, luck, positivity, and protection; filters air and removes indoor air pollutants

WILLOW: Creativity, fertility, health, hope, lunar energy, and safety; treats headaches and aches and pains

Pay Attention to the Energy of the Universe

There is so much more to green witchcraft than connecting with plants and honoring Mother Earth. The broader universe has a profound impact on our little blue planet, and those energies are often incorporated into a green witch's magical and healing practice. Green witches recognize and honor the changing seasons, and we also use the moon, sun, stars, and elements to enhance spell work. You can even harness the power of the weather to enact change.

As with all paths in witchcraft, no two green witches are alike. Some, like me, may ignore astrology and focus on magical allies like the changing seasons and moon phases. Some may live in areas where seasonal changes are less noticeable or consistent, and therefore choose to rely more heavily on astrology instead. No matter what you decide, recognizing the impact of the broader universe can be transformative for your magical practice.

The Seasons

Seasons look very different depending on where you live in the world. Nonetheless, the earth's revolution around the sun can cause even the smallest shifts, the energies of which can be harnessed in your magical practice. Those living farther from the equator likely experience four seasons: spring, summer, fall, and winter. Spring is associated with rebirth and fertility, summer with strength and abundance, fall with change and death, and winter with rest and self-reflection. For those near the equator, you may experience only two seasons: rainy and dry. The rainy season corresponds with abundance, prosperity, and rebirth, and the dry season corresponds to death, rest, and self-reflection. Tailoring your remedies, rituals, and spells to seasonal changes will amplify your intention and help you live in harmony with the earth.

The Phases of the Moon

The moon has been associated with mysticism and witchcraft for centuries, representing transformation, intuition, dreams, prophecy, and emotions. It takes the moon 29.5 days to complete a full lunar cycle. During this cycle, each phase of the moon has different energies and correspondences that can be used to power your remedies, rituals, and spells. The moon phases and their correspondences are:

Dark moon: Rest, banishing, binding, divination, and shadow work

New moon: New beginnings and intention setting

Waxing moon: Attraction, luck, wealth, and success; drawing things toward you

Full moon: Charging, healing, clarity, and protection

Waning moon: Banishing, ridding illness, and breaking habits; drawing things away from you

The Sun and Other Stars

Like the moon, the sun and stars can be used in your practice to enhance your remedies, rituals, and spells. The sun has the most profound impact on our planet. Without the sun, life would not exist as we know it, and our planet would be a cold barren rock. The sun corresponds with courage, health, joy, luck, passion, strength, success, and wealth. It can be used to empower charms and talismans, create sun water, or soothe depression.

The stars and constellations, however, have a lesser impact on our planet and therefore impact our magic in more subtle ways. They are often observed in conjunction with other planetary movements and are believed to impact our personalities.

The Elements

Throughout history, there have been various understandings of the elements. Modern neopaganism recognizes four primary elements: air, earth, fire, and water. Some traditions include a fifth element known as spirit or ether. These elements all work in harmony to comprise the earth, and therefore play an important role in modern green witchcraft and self-care. Infuse your remedies, rituals, and spells with each of these elements, or call upon them to enhance your intention and healing. Below is a brief description of each element's correspondence.

Air: Clarity, wisdom, knowledge, and thought

Earth: Grounding, strength, stability, healing, and success

Fire: Energy, passion, destruction, power, and courage

Spirit or Ether: Selflessness, mercy, transformation, transcendence, and self-awareness

Water: Emotion, intuition, self-healing, fertility, and reflection

The Weather

Weather is a culmination of the positive and negative aspects of all elements. For much of history, humans have sought to control the weather—whether it be calling for rain or tying up bad weather to ensure safe travel. The modern green witch, however, doesn't seek to control the weather. Instead, they live in harmony with it, using it to create powerful remedies, rituals, and spells. The destructive energies of thunderstorms can be harnessed and used in your spell work. Clear, sunny afternoons can be used to charge charms, stones, talismans, and water with joy and luck. Water from light rains can be used to heal, nourish, and restore. The possibilities are endless.

YULE

SAMHAIN

IMBOLC

December 21 February 2

October 31 March 21

MABON

OSTARA

September 21 May 1

August 1 June 21

LUGHNASADH

BELTANE

LITHA

The Wheel of the Year

The Wheel of the Year is a modern take on ancient pagan holidays and festivals, combining a number of cultures into one cohesive yearly cycle. The Wheel of the Year is made up of eight festivals, or sabbats, that occur around the same time every year. Four of the sabbats, known as quarter days, are solar events. These include the solstices and equinoxes, also known as Ostara, Litha, Mabon, and Yule. The other four, known as cross-quarter days, fall between the solar events and mark transitions in the seasons and agriculture. These include Beltane, Imbolc, Lughnasadh/Lammas, and Samhain. The green witch can use the Wheel of the Year as a tool to keep track of the seasons and planetary movements, and ultimately to help them live in harmony with the earth.

Each of the eight sabbats has different correspondences and folklore, so each is used for different magical and healing intentions. The eight sabbats and their correspondences are:

IMBOLC: Awakening, initiation, and new life

OSTARA: Balance, fertility, growth, and rebirth

BELTANE: Creativity, passion, and pleasure

LITHA: Abundance, energy, and joy

LUGHNASADH/LAMMAS: Blessings, growth, and prosperity

MABON: Community, gratitude, and transition

SAMHAIN: Death, destruction, and spirit/ancestor work

YULE: Light, hope, and renewal

Additional Tools for the Green Witch

Just like cooking, green witchcraft uses a specific set of tools. Apart from natural ingredients, green witches often make use of brooms, jars and bowls, a mortar and pestle, pendulums and dowsing rods, tarot cards or runes, wands, and other such magical items. These items are often found, made, repurposed, or purchased from local consignment stores, when magically appropriate. Having tools on hand can certainly make your practice easier, but they are never strictly necessary. The tools do not make an act magical—you do. Tools are simply a way to direct your energies, store spell ingredients, or make communication with spirits easier. This section features a non-exhaustive list of tools that will help you perform or create the remedies, rituals, and spells found in part 2. Feel free to explore other tools and include them in your practice as well. Make your practice your own.

Broom

The broom, also known as a besom, has a long and rich history in witchcraft too extensive to detail completely here. Brooms are most famously known as the vehicle we ride on to the Witches' Sabbath. In reality, brooms are used most often to sweep away unwanted and negative energies, protect against evil spirits, and mark times of transition. I suggest having one broom for mundane cleaning and a separate cleansed and consecrated besom for magical work. The broom is a powerful tool for maintaining a healthy, happy home. It makes the perfect companion for the green witch just starting out on their healing and self-care journey.

Jars and Bowls

Jars and bowls are a witch's best friend. They are used to store magical ingredients and create oil infusions, moon water, sun water, teas, and tinctures. Jars and other small glass bottles are also used to create spell jars and witch bottles, which have historically been used for protection and sometimes cursing.

Bowls can also be used for storage, but they are more commonly used for holding offerings, divination, or burning incense and spell ingredients (if fire-safe). Bowls can also be used as an integral part of a spell, as in incantation bowls and many water spells. The color and material of your bowl can aid in your spell work as well. For example, silver bowls can infuse spells with lunar energy.

Mortar and Pestle

The roots of the mortar and pestle date back to early herbalism, pharmacology, and food preparation. The mortar and pestle were historically used to grind and blend ingredients such as herbs, roots, spices, eggshells, resins, and even meat. Today the mortar and pestle are used by witches for the same purposes, aiding in the creation of candle dressings, herbal remedies, incense, spell powders, teas, and other magical concoctions.

Before using your new mortar and pestle, season it to remove any leftover grit from the manufacturer. Begin by cleaning it with warm water (no soap!). Dry completely and grind 2 or 3 tablespoons of rice into a fine powder. Repeat three to five times, then rinse with warm water. It's now ready for use!

Pendulums and Dowsing Rods

Pendulums and dowsing rods are both tools for dowsing, a form of divination used to detect something hidden. Historically, these tools have been used to find water, minerals, lost objects, and even treasure. They can also be used to find sources of illness and communicate with spirits. Pendulums are composed of a suspended weight attached to a chain or thread. Dowsing rods, on the other hand, are Y-shaped branches made of hazel, rowan, or willow, although any magical tree can be used. Witches hold pendulums and dowsing rods lightly and track their motions to find whatever they are looking for. They can be used in your healing and self-care practice to find sources of disease and hurt, helping you to pinpoint exactly where you need to heal.

Tarot Cards and Runes

Tarot cards and runes are tools of divination that have been used for centuries. Tarot card decks generally include cards from two categories: Major Arcana and Minor Arcana. The twenty-two Major Arcana cards represent life lessons, overarching themes, and influences in your life. The fifty-six Minor Arcana cards contain four suits, similar to regular playing cards, and represent the everyday choices and actions we face. Runes are used in much the same way as tarot, but they are composed of twenty-four letters. Both of these divination methods can be used to offer advice and suggestions. They can also be used to bring specific energies to a spell, enhance the healing properties of a remedy, or offer healing lessons to meditate on.

Wand

Wands, much like the broom, are an iconic occult symbol deeply associated with magic and witchcraft. Throughout history, they were generally made from tree branches, and the magical properties of the tree would infuse the wand with specific energies. Today, wands are often made from various materials, including bone, clay, crystals, glass, horns, pine cones, wood, and even plastic, although I suggest avoiding plastic whenever possible. Wands are used to concentrate, store, and direct energy for magical and healing purposes. Many ancient healers believed illness was caused by evil spirits, so they would use wands to cast out spirits before using their herbal remedies. Wands can be used the same way in your modern healing practice, as well as for casting protecting spells and warding off evil spirits.

Growing a Garden at Home

Growing your own ingredients at home is a great way to strengthen your connection with the natural world. You can also make the acquisition of certain ingredients more affordable by growing them in a garden, window box, or small planters. Growing your own plants provides you with opportunities to connect with the spirits of plant allies, create a serene place to meditate, purify the air in your home, and bring the healing energies of Mother Earth directly to you.

When starting your own garden, preparation is everything. How much space do you have? How many hours of sunlight does the space receive? Are you growing in the ground or in containers? What plants grow well in these conditions? And most important, what is your budget? Starting a garden does not have to be expensive. In fact, most dollar stores sell planters, soil, and seeds in the spring and summer months. Old jars, milk jugs, and tea tins also make great windowsill planters. To get started, pour boiled water into your soil to sterilize and hydrate it. Then fortify your soil with homemade compost made from a mixture of water, banana peels, coffee grounds, and powdered eggshells. Plant your seeds directly into the soil and watch as your garden grows.

Setting Up an Altar

When you set up an altar or create a sacred space, you create a space that exists outside the mundane world. This space will aid you in your green witchcraft and self-care practice, allowing you a safe arena to conduct your magic and healing. These spaces are not strictly necessary, but they are helpful. Entering your unique space can act as a trigger to get you into a magical mindset. Creating an altar or sacred space is super easy and can be completely inconspicuous.

1. Find a place that is conducive to your spell work and self-care. This could be a dresser, bedside table, or even a tree stump. Find someplace private so you won't be disturbed, but also someplace you can easily bring your tools and ingredients.

2. Cleanse and consecrate the space. This can be done through smoke cleansing, bell ringing, or chanting. I prefer to smoke cleanse using rosemary or pine resin, which are known for cleansing and protecting.

3. Intuitively decorate your altar. I place candles, fresh flowers, bowls of water and soil, stones, bones, and other found objects on my altar. Many of these items are inconspicuous and can be arranged to look like nothing more than a pretty display.

Whatever you decide, your altar should be distinctly *you*. There are no rules, so go with what works best for you and your magic.

Keeping a Journal or Grimoire

The key to being a successful green witch and creating a sustainable self-care practice is journaling and record-keeping. Most witches keep a grimoire or a journal, also known as a Book of Shadows, to document their progress and spell work. This is a great way to keep notes on specific ingredients, tools, phases of the moon, seasonal changes, and any other areas of interest. This also acts as a resource for creating your very own spells and rituals. Keeping a detailed record allows you to reflect on your successes and failures as a witch. Successful spells can be used in the future, and unsuccessful ones can be used as learning experiences. Record-keeping also helps you break a spell in case it backfires. When recording remedies, rituals, and spells, be sure to include the purpose/goal, date, time, moon phase, spell length, ingredients, deities/spirits worked with, actions performed, words spoken, unusual occurrences, location of spell remains, and results.

Apart from record-keeping, journaling will aid you on your healing journey. Use your journal to process trauma, grief, and other bothersome thoughts and emotions. Examining these feelings on paper will help relieve stress and increase self-awareness. Write freely about your day or feelings or explore journaling prompts if you're not sure where to begin.

Prioritize Cleansing and Organizing Before You Begin

It's essential to cleanse and charge your space and ingredients before starting any spell work or healing rituals, including the remedies, rituals, and spells in part 2. Proper cleansing and charging ensure the energy is conducive to spell casting, healing, and self-care. How you cleanse your space and ingredients is completely up to you. Popular methods include smoke cleansing, saining (blessing), asperging, bell ringing, chanting, or even blowing. When smoke cleansing, choose plants associated with cleansing and purification, such as rosemary, juniper, lavender, frankincense, myrrh, and thyme. Keep in mind that each of these plants have other correspondences in addition to cleansing. For example, lavender not only cleanses, but also calms. It's the perfect herb to burn prior to taking a relaxing bath or going to bed. Rosemary, associated with memory and reflection, is perfect to use before journaling or doing shadow work. Sound is another cleansing method. Sound is great for spells and rituals meant to uplift energy or dispel depression or anxiety, because sound clears the space and raises your own energy. Another method, blowing, infuses your objects with your intention as well as cleanses them. Not all items need to be cleansed—let your intuition guide you in your preparatory practices.

Center Your Mind and Clarify Your Intentions

To ensure your work goes as planned, it is of the utmost importance to enter any witchcraft practice with clear intentions. Before engaging in any of the remedies, rituals, and spells found in part 2, you should ground, center, and set your intention. Centering yourself helps you concentrate your energy and focus on your goal. Being in the moment also helps clarify your intentions, preventing your mundane thoughts from infiltrating your true desires. It's impossible to engage in deep self-reflection, for instance, if you are worried about cooking dinner. Time and quiet are not always available resources, but taking this intentional step if you are able will put you in a magical mindset conducive to spell work and healing.

Grounding is the act of connecting with the earth to stabilize and release energy. This can be accomplished through many different methods including earthing, meditation, breathing exercises, and even dancing. Earthing is my grounding method of choice, as it connects you directly to Mother Earth. To earth, plant your feet or hands firmly on the ground, preferably outside, or in a bowl of dirt. Close your eyes and visualize roots sprouting from you and growing deep into the ground. See your energies intertwining as you absorb the balancing and stabilizing energies of the earth and release your anxieties, fears, and frustrations.

Nature Is the Ultimate Teacher to Heal Yourself

At the end of the day, nature is the ultimate teacher for healing and self-care. Despite all that Mother Earth has been through, she always manages to overcome even the most cataclysmic events, and just when things seem darkest, the light returns. In most cases, our bodies, much like Mother Earth, are designed to do the same if we give them the chance. Exploring common ingredients and tools of green witchcraft, as well as learning to tap into and pay attention to the natural world, are all great first steps toward healing in harmony with the earth. Listen to nature and learn to slow down, accept change, and persevere in the face of adversity. Our planet provides not only lessons but remedies as well, from medicinal plants and grounding stones to cleansing waters and invigorating sunlight. All of these can be incorporated into your witchcraft, healing, and self-care.

Nature has much to teach us, but it is not a cure-all. You must be an active participant in your healing journey, working to remove yourself from toxic relationships and situations, engaging in shadow work and self-reflection, and seeking medical advice and therapy when needed. Remember to prioritize your needs and be consistent. Self-care and healing take work and time. Note that the healing methods in this book should not be used in place of professional medical care. If you are experiencing health issues, always consult a trusted doctor or other medical professional.

Key Takeaways

In this chapter, we learned about the basic ingredients, tools, and practices of the green witch. We also explored ways to respectfully gather items, cleanse your space and objects, and keep a magical journal. Common ingredients used by the green witch include plants, crystals and stones, essential oils, candles, and incense. Green witches also recognize and honor the changing seasons, use the moon, sun, and stars, and harness the power of the weather to enact change. Additional tools used in green witchcraft include the mortar and pestle, jars and bowls, brooms, tarot cards and runes, and pendulums and dowsing rods.

◆ When gathering items, ask permission before taking and leave behind an offering as thanks.

◆ Each tool used in green witchcraft has its own unique magical and healing properties, which can be used for specific purposes and spell work.

◆ Growing your own ingredients at home helps connect you with the natural world and makes the acquisition of certain ingredients more affordable.

◆ Keep track of your work in a journal or grimoire to record your progress and engage in self-reflection.

◆ You should cleanse, ground, and center before engaging in any spell work or self-care.

II

PART II

A-to-Z Natural Remedies, Rituals, and Spells for Self-Care

In this part, you will find fifty-five natural remedies, rituals, and spells to aid you on your healing and self-care journey. Each addresses a common challenge or ailments in one of the following categories: mind, body, spirit, home, and community. This part is organized alphabetically by these challenges, from abundance to spiritual blockages. To ensure everyone can benefit, they incorporate natural ingredients most people will have on hand or can easily access. Some activities will feature several different ingredient options to choose from. Remember, I am writing from my personal experience and cultural background. If there are other ingredients that hold more significance to you, I encourage you to use those. Feel free to research and adjust these remedies, rituals, and spells to suit your own needs and spiritual sensibilities. Healing and self-care should be tailored to you. So, what are you waiting for? Let's dive in!

ABUNDANCE BOWL

Perpetual lack of basic necessities increases your risk of disease and mental illness. Abundance is defined as having a large quantity of something such as money, food, or happiness. This spell bowl, along with mundane work, will help ensure you never go without. Rice is associated with stability and abundance, particularly related to food. Cinnamon and pyrite are associated with financial abundance, and mint is associated with general abundance and good health. Lemons help remove blockages, cleanse a space, and bring happiness to the space. Create this spell bowl during the waxing or full moon.

Shallow bowl, about 5 inches in diameter

Dried rice, enough to fill the bowl 1 inch deep

Pyrite

1 teaspoon ground cinnamon

1 teaspoon crushed dried mint leaves

1 tablespoon crushed or finely chopped dried lemon peel

1. Cleanse the bowl using your preferred cleansing method.

2. Pour the rice into the bowl while saying:

    "My family always has enough food."

3. With your finger, draw a spiral in the rice, starting in the center and moving clockwise around the bowl.

4. Place the pyrite in the center of the rice. Sprinkle the cinnamon throughout the spiral you created while saying:

    "My family always has enough money."

5. Next, sprinkle the mint throughout the spiral while saying:

    "My family is always in good health."

6. Next sprinkle the dried lemon peel throughout the spiral while saying:

   "My family is always happy and joyous."

7. Hold the bowl in both hands and say:

   "My family is blessed with abundance."

8. Place the bowl in your kitchen or on your altar. Refresh the bowl when you feel your abundance waning.

ANCESTRAL TRAUMA
TAROT SPREAD

Ancestral trauma, as discussed on page 18, is hereditary trauma that's passed down from generation to generation. Ancestral trauma can manifest in many ways, including mental illness, increased risk of addiction, memory loss, hypervigilance, and unresolved grief. Assessing the situation is a great first step toward healing ancestral trauma and breaking cycles. This tarot spread will help you identify what trauma exists in your family line and what your ancestors suggest you do about it.

Matches or lighter
Incense associated with your
  ancestors

Tarot deck
Writing utensil
Notebook or journal

1. Begin by sitting comfortably where you will not be disturbed.

2. Light your incense and shuffle your tarot deck, keeping your intention firmly in your mind.

3. Spread the deck in front of you and draw six cards. Place them faceup in a single row in front of you, starting on the left and moving right.

4. Interpret the meaning of each card using the following guide. Feel free to look up the meanings of your cards or use your intuition as your guide:

   CARD 1: What ancestral trauma or cycle needs to be broken?

   CARD 2: How does this trauma or cycle affect my life?

   CARD 3: What can I do to heal my ancestral line?

   CARD 4: What energy do I need to draw on to begin to release and heal?

   CARD 5: What cycle will begin if I break this trauma or cycle?

   CARD 6: How can I honor my ancestors moving forward?

5. Record your findings in a notebook or journal and use what you learned to help you begin your healing journey.

ANGER RELEASE SPELL

Anger is one of those tricky emotions that can quickly get us into trouble. It should be noted, however, that anger is a valid emotion. Let yourself sit with your anger as needed, but don't let it consume you. This quick spell uses an ice cube or amethyst to cool hot tempers and leave you clear-minded.

Ice cube or amethyst crystal

1. Take a deep breath through your nose and exhale through your mouth.

2. Place the ice cube or amethyst against your third eye and say:

   "Calm my enraged mind."

3. Visualize your anger leaving you and entering the object. Next, place it on your lips and say:

   "Freeze my raging tongue."

4. Repeat the visualization. Next, place it against your heart and say:

   "Cool my storming heart."

5. Repeat the visualization. Hold the object firmly in your hand, visualizing all your anger soaking into it. If using an ice cube, let it melt completely.

ANTIANXIETY SPELL JAR

According to the Mayo Clinic, anxiety disorders are charac-terized by "intense, excessive and persistent worry and fear about everyday situations." With social media, global health crises, and the promotion of rugged individualism, it's no surprise that human beings struggle with anxiety. This spell jar employs the calming properties of lavender, chamomile, and roses to help ease symptoms of anxiety. Perform this spell during the waxing or full moon and follow it up by reaching out to a licensed therapist.

Small jar with lid or cork
Dried lavender
Dried chamomile
Dried rose petals
Amethyst crystal chips (small enough to fit into jar)

2 or 3 drops moon water
2 or 3 drops honey
Blue candle
Match or lighter

1. Begin by cleansing your small jar or vial using your preferred cleansing method.

2. In the jar, combine the lavender, chamomile, rose petals, amethyst, moon water, and honey. Seal with blue wax from the candle.

3. Hold the jar in both hands near your heart and recite the following enchantment:

   "Bring me peace, serenity, and calm.
   Anxiety, I will you to be gone.
   Calm my thoughts and soothe my mind,
   Leave not a trace of anxiety behind."

4. Carry the jar on your person or place in a location where you will see it often.

I'M SORRY SPELL

Arguments with friends and family often leave us feeling guilty and hurt. When you find yourself on the wrong side of an argument, it's best to recognize what you did wrong and apologize without blame or strings attached. If you are struggling to formulate an apology, this spell uses white tulips to help you attract forgiveness. Sorry *is an incredibly powerful word capable of great magic, but only if you mean it.*

2 (3-inch) pieces of heart-shaped fabric, preferably pink

Pink or white thread

Needle

Pillow stuffing

4-by-4-inch piece of paper

Writing utensil

Rose quartz or rhodonite crystal chips

Rose petals

White tulip petals

1. Begin by grounding and cleansing your items using your preferred cleansing method.

2. Place the two pieces of fabric, print side facing each other, and stitch along the edge, leaving at least 1 or 2 inches open to fill. As you stitch, chant, "I mend the bonds that have been broken."

3. Turn the sewn fabric right-side out and add a small amount of pillow stuffing to the bottom, leaving some extra room.

4. On the piece of paper, write your name and that of the person to whom you wish to make amends. Fold the paper in half so the names face each other and place it on top of the stuffing, in the center of the pillow.

5. Add crystal chips and flower petals, keeping your intention firmly in your mind.

6. Finish stitching the pillow shut and hold it in both hands. Fill it with your love.

7. Apologize to the person to whom you wish to make amends and give them the pillow.

DENDROTHERAPY TO BALANCE YOUR SPIRIT

You may have heard green witches referred to as tree huggers, and that description couldn't be more accurate. Not only do green witches seek to preserve and protect Mother Earth, but we also literally hug trees. Trees are extremely magical and have enormous capacity to give and receive energy. This process is known as dendrotherapy. Much like hugging someone you love, hugging trees has also been shown to reduce stress and increase dopamine and serotonin, the hormones associated with happiness. If you are feeling spiritually drained, confused, or hesitant, use this short ritual to help balance your spirit. When picking a tree, be mindful of the energies it projects—try to align with a tree that is willing to help.

Living tree, preferably oak, pine, birch, or willow

Eco-friendly offering, such as saliva, water, or a crystal

1. Find a secluded tree where you will not be disturbed.

2. Plant your feet firmly on the ground and place your hands on the tree. Close your eyes and feel the energy from the tree. Reach your consciousness out to it and ask the tree if it would be willing to help balance your spirit.

3. If the answer is yes, embrace the tree. Steady your breathing. Let your insecurities, anger, sadness, and other unwanted emotions leave you, being replaced by loving, healing energies. Visualize your spirit being realigned and balanced.

4. Continue embracing the tree until you feel completely balanced and refreshed.

5. When finished, thank the tree for its assistance and leave your offering at its base.

CANDLE RITUAL TO SET FIRM BOUNDARIES

Setting healthy boundaries helps boost self-esteem, develops independence, reduces stress, and helps bring life into focus. Saying no is a great way to begin setting boundaries, but if you are a people pleaser like me, you may struggle to do so. This simple ritual will help you set boundaries and should be followed up with real-world action. Amazonite fortifies personal boundaries, hematite emotional boundaries, and kyanite relationship boundaries. Lemon balm helps your message be heard.

Fire-safe dish
Sand (enough to cover the
   bottom of your dish)
2 white candles
Toothpick
Match or lighter

Amazonite crystal
Hematite crystal
Kyanite crystal
1 or 2 teaspoons dried
   lemon balm

1. Begin by filling the bottom of the fire-safe dish with sand.

2. On one candle, use the toothpick to write your name. On the other, write the name of what you wish to set boundaries with.

3. Place the candles opposite each other in the fire-safe dish and light them.

4. Draw a line in the sand between them, stating aloud the boundary you wish to set.

5. Place the crystals along the drawn boundary and recite the following incantation:

   "With amazonite, hematite, and kyanite, I reinforce my boundary."

6. Sprinkle the lemon balm around the edge of the dish, encircling the candles and boundary while saying the following incantation:

   "The boundary is laid. I shall be heard and respected."

7. Visualize the boundary you have set manifesting.

8. When your visualization is complete, snuff out the candles.

9. Relight the candles the following day and repeat the visualization. Repeat each day for 3 days or until the candles burn down completely.

BRAIN FOG BEGONE TEA

Brain fog is a mental phenomenon characterized by feeling confused, forgetful, and overwhelmed. It can be caused by lack of sleep, stress, and overworking. This tea will help alleviate these symptoms. Green tea contains caffeine to stimulate the mind, and ginkgo, peppermint, and gotu kola improve overall brain function.

Mortar and pestle

2 teaspoons loose-leaf green tea
   (or 2 tea bags)

1 teaspoon dried ginkgo leaf
   (or 1 tea bag)

½ teaspoon dried peppermint

1 teaspoon dried gotu kola
   (or 1 tea bag) (optional)

Tea ball or strainer

Heat-safe drinking vessel

1 cup hot water (180°F/82°C)

¼ cup oat milk

Sweetener, to taste

1. In the mortar and pestle, grind the herbs until they are well combined.

2. Add the herbal mixture to the tea ball and place in the drinking vessel. Pour the hot water over the mixture. Steep for 5 minutes, then remove the mixture.

3. Add the oat milk and sweetener and stir counterclockwise.

4. Drink, feeling the warmth of the tea clearing the fog, leaving you alert and clear-headed.

CALM   CATEGORY: MIND

FLAME MEDITATION
TO CALM THE MIND

Quieting the mind is difficult for most people. It can be especially challenging if you are neurodivergent or extremely stressed. Learning to meditate, even lightly, can aid you in both your witchcraft and healing journey bolster. Meditation bolsters magic, reduces stress, and improves focus. This meditation uses the flame of a candle to help you reach a calming, meditative state. The flame acts as an external point of focus and provides a fixed point to turn back to if your mind or eyes begin to wander. This can be particularly helpful for those with ADHD or any attention difficulties. Light blue, lavender, and chamomile are associated with peace and calm, and mint improves focus.

Toothpick
Light blue or white candle
Mortar and pestle
½ teaspoon dried lavender
½ teaspoon dried chamomile

½ teaspoon dried mint
Plate
2 or 3 drops olive oil
Match or lighter

1. Begin by sitting in a comfortable position where you will not be disturbed.

2. Using the toothpick, carve a symbol you associate with calm, such as a peace sign or Othala (rune), into the candle.

3. Using a mortar and pestle, grind the herbs until well combined and pour onto a plate.

CONTINUED

4. Anoint the candle with oil, rubbing to coat the sides of the candle. Make sure the symbol you carved is well coated.

5. Roll the candle in the herbs until the entire candle and symbol are lightly coated.

6. Light the candle and take a deep breath. Focus on the movement of the flame and slow your breath. Allow your mind to quiet and your eyes to shift out of focus.

7. Remain focused on the candle flame for 5 to 30 minutes.

MAGICAL ALL-PURPOSE CLEANER

Your personal health and wellness benefits from a clean home, both mundanely and magically. When we keep a dirty home, it clutters our minds, overwhelms our senses, and even causes physical illness and disease. This magic-infused, all-purpose cleaner will help you clean away dirt and debris, as well as remove negative and unwanted energies. White vinegar and lemons are associated with protection and banishment and help to effectively remove unwanted energy and entities (including insects). Lemons are uplifting and fresh, leaving positive energies behind. Lavender and rosemary bring peace, harmony, and clarity, as well as general protection. This cleaner is safe for most surfaces and should be made during the full moon, which is associated with protection and empowerment.

1-quart mason jar

1 lemon, sliced

1 cup distilled white vinegar

Funnel

Glass spray bottle

¾ cup distilled water

¼ cup rubbing alcohol

10 drops lavender essential oil*

5 drops rosemary essential oil*

1. In the mason jar, combine the lemon slices and vinegar. Seal the jar and store in a cool, dry place for 1 to 3 weeks.

2. Using a funnel, strain the lemon-infused vinegar into a glass spray bottle. Add water, alcohol, and essential oils.

CONTINUED

3. Replace the cap on the bottle and shake until well combined, visualizing the mixture filling with bright golden, purifying light.

4. While cleaning with this spray, visualize the dust, dirt, debris, and negativity being cleansed and removed from your space. You may also chant the following enchantment:

"With lemon, rosemary, and lavender, I remove all dirt and debris. Leave nothing but happiness and positivity behind."

*If you don't have access to essential oils, replace them with 1 or 2 tablespoons fresh herbs and add them during step 1.

CLEANSING BODY SCRUB

Taking care of your skin is a vital part of any wellness routine. This body scrub is a powerful tool that helps clean, exfoliate, and moisturize skin. It can also fight acne and remove any spiritual filth, bad luck, and stagnant energy hanging around you. Coffee grounds contain caffeine, which stimulates blood flow and reduces puffiness. Sugar helps draw positive energy toward you, and salt acts as a cleanser and purifier, removing unwanted energies. Rosemary and lemon are both associated with protection and act as astringents to reduce acne and control oil production. Finally, coconut oil helps nourish and moisturize and is magically associated with healing and protection. Combined, these ingredients create a cleansing and protective body scrub that will leave you feeling refreshed and invigorated!

16-ounce mason jar with lid
½ cup coffee grounds
¼ cup sugar
2 tablespoons coarse salt

1 tablespoon rosemary leaves or
   3 drops rosemary essential oil
Juice of ½ lemon
¼ cup melted coconut oil

1. In the jar, combine the coffee grounds, sugar, salt, and rosemary. Stir counterclockwise, envisioning the departure of illness, fatigue, and anything else you wish to be cleansed from your life.

2. Add the lemon juice and melted coconut oil to the dry mixture. This time, stir clockwise and envision your life being full of health, wellness, and happiness.

3. Take a warm shower or bath and gently rub the scrub counterclockwise over your body, visualizing yourself being cleansed of physical and spiritual debris. Rinse.

ROOM-CLEANSING RITUAL

It might be time for a deep energy cleanse if you are feeling run-down, getting sick often, or having trouble sleeping. If you find that your home or living space is full of strife and conflict, use this cleansing ritual to reset the energy and begin again with a clean slate. Onions are deep energy cleansers. Salt and white candles are used for purification. This ritual will leave your space completely cleansed of all energies, so it's important to follow up with a spell to invite uplifting energies back.

Fire-safe dish for each room	**Salt**
Half an onion for each room	**Match or lighter**
White tealight for each room	**Bell**

1. Before beginning this ritual, completely clean all clutter, dirt, and debris in your home.

2. Start at the back of your home. On a fire-safe dish, place an onion half and a white tealight, then create a ring of salt around them. Open any windows or doors and light the white candle.

3. Walk counterclockwise around the room while ringing your bell and saying the following enchantment:

   "By air, earth, fire, and water, energy begone.
   Leave this place. Flee from my home. Leave not a trace.
   So I will it, so it is."

4. Allow the candle to burn out completely, then repeat the process in each room using new ingredients.

5. When you have completed the ritual, throw the remains of the spell in the trash outside of your home.

SPACE-CLEARING HERBAL BLEND

When we engage in healing and self-care activities, many feelings and energies can arise. Because of this, it is often a good idea to reset and rebalance before and after. Clearing a space of unwanted energies is a great way to reset. This herbal blend can be burned as an incense or simmered for a smokeless cleansing method. Myrrh and rosemary are naturally cleansing and purifying, as well as protective in nature. Cinnamon is uplifting and rejuvenates a space that has just been cleared. Lavender is relaxing, reduces stress, and brings positivity to the space.

FOR THE INCENSE:

Mortar and pestle

½ teaspoon myrrh resin

½ teaspoon to 1 teaspoon dried rosemary

½ teaspoon to 1 teaspoon ground cinnamon

½ teaspoon to 1 teaspoon dried lavender flowers

Fire-safe dish

Charcoal disk

Match or lighter

FOR THE SIMMER POT:

10 drops myrrh essential oil

½ teaspoon to 1 teaspoon dried rosemary

½ teaspoon to 1 teaspoon ground cinnamon

½ teaspoon to 1 teaspoon dried lavender flowers

Fire-safe pot

2 cups water

CONTINUED

TO MAKE THE INCENSE:

1. In the mortar and pestle, combine the resin and herbs and grind well. As you grind, visualize the mixture filling with cleansing energy.

2. Light the charcoal and place it in a fire-safe dish. Sprinkle a small amount of loose incense on the charcoal.

3. Place in the location you wish to clear or walk around the room. Add more incense as needed.

TO CREATE THE SIMMER POT:

4. Combine the essential oil and herbs with water in a pot and bring to a boil.

5. Reduce heat and simmer until liquid is reduced by half.

STOP THE GOSSIP SPELL

Gossip and rumors can be so disruptive and stressful—especially if the gossip is about you. Use this simple spell to stop gossip dead in its tracks and take your name out of someone else's mouth. This spell "ties" the gossip up, using twine, thread, yarn, or ribbon. If you don't have something to tie up your spell, you can place the paper in a container with water and freeze it, thus freezing the gossip. Because you will be burying the remains of this spell, they will degrade over time, releasing the magic you performed. Should the gossip continue some weeks or months later, repeat the spell. For best results, perform this spell during the waning or dark moon.

Sheet of paper
Writing utensil

Biodegradable twine, thread, yarn, or ribbon, preferably black
Trowel

1. On the sheet of paper, write the name of the person who is gossiping about you. If you are unaware of where the gossip is coming from, simply write the word *gossip* on the paper.

2. Fold the paper away from you two or three times.

3. Using the black twine, thread, yarn, or ribbon, wrap the folded paper nine times while saying the following enchantment:

   "No more shall your wicked tongue wag,
   I bind the gossip with this tag.
   No longer shall you speak of me,
   So I will it, so shall it be."

4. Dig a hole, outside or in a potted plant, and bury the paper and thread.

TALISMAN TO IMPROVE COMMUNICATION

Communication is difficult. It can be especially difficult if you feel nervous or upset, are struggling with social cues, or are dealing with somebody who is not particularly open and receptive. In most scenarios, however, communication is a worthy task. Open and honest communication helps forge stronger relationships and reduces stress and anxiety. This can be incredibly important when seeking to heal past trauma or advocate for social change. Create this talisman to help you achieve a specific communication goal. If you are looking to speak your truth but avoid conflict, use sodalite. If you are looking to speak from a place of power or wisdom, use amazonite or labradorite. If you are looking to amplify and strengthen your voice, use clear quartz or blue kyanite. If you need help speaking eloquently, create your talisman on Wednesday. If you are looking to speak with wisdom and ensure victory, create it on Tuesday.

Crystal of your choosing—
  amazonite, blue kyanite,
  labradorite, quartz, or sodalite

Match or lighter
Frankincense incense

1. Begin by cleansing the crystal using your preferred cleansing method.

2. Light the incense and hold the crystal in your hand, feeling it warm in your hand as you focus on your intention. Blow your intention into the crystal or state it out loud.

3. Pass the crystal through the incense while reciting the following enchantment:

"My words flow freely and clearly from my mouth. I am heard and understood."

4. Carry or wear the crystal on your person to improve communication.

SELF-CONFIDENCE ESSENTIAL OIL BLEND

I don't know about you, but I am often plagued by self-doubt. Imposter syndrome leaves me feeling like a fraud more often than not, even in situations where I know I am more than qualified. To fight those feelings of self-doubt, I often turn to confidence-boosting smells to help reprogram my brain. Before you head into an interview, presentation, or other stress-inducing situation, apply a small amount of this essential oil blend to your wrists and temples to boost your confidence and ensure success. Citrus smells like sweet orange and grapefruit fight fear and increase boldness. Bergamot and jasmine banish self-doubt and increase creativity, and ginger restores determination. It should be noted that sweet orange, grapefruit, bergamot, and jasmine essential oils are unsafe for pets, so exercise caution when using.

10-ml roller bottle or bottle with lid

4 drops sweet orange essential oil*

4 drops grapefruit essential oil*

2 drops bergamot essential oil*

2 drops ginger essential oil*

1 drop jasmine essential oil*

Crystal chip of your choosing—citrine, tiger's eye, or carnelian, small enough to fit into the bottle

Carrier oil, such as grapeseed oil, to fill the bottle

1. In the roller bottle, combine the essential oils and crystal chip and top with your carrier oil of choice. Seal the bottle.

2. Gently roll the bottle between your hands while saying the following enchantment:

   "Oils distilled from Mother Earth,
   Boost my confidence, strength, and mirth."

3. Visualize the oil blend filling with bright orange light, the color of confidence and success.

4. Apply as needed.

   *If you don't have access to essential oils, this recipe can be modified to create an oil infusion using fresh or dried herbs. Combine 2 parts dried orange peel, 2 parts dried grapefruit peel, 1 part dried ginger, and 1 part dried jasmine in a small mason jar. Cover with olive oil, replace the lid, and place in a sunny place for 4 weeks. Shake daily. Strain the oil to remove herbs and store in a dark glass jar.

CONNECTING WITH YOUR GENIUS LOCI

Connecting with your local land spirits is a great way to build a sense of community and find magical allies. Many of these spirits are more reserved due to environmental trauma, but they can be reached, and a relationship can be cultivated. In seeking such relationships, you rewild your soul, break your connection with the individualistic nature of capitalism, and heal the bonds between humans and the land. Green witches are stewards of the land, and healing means healing the wounds we have inflicted on Mother Earth.

**Eco-friendly offering, such as
   water, stones, fruit, or honey**

1. Find a spot, preferably outdoors, where you will not be disturbed.

2. Plant your feet firmly on the ground and visualize your connection to the earth. Feel roots sprouting from the bottoms of your feet, growing deep into the soil.

3. When your connection to the earth is complete, state that you wish to connect with the local land spirit. Look for signs that the spirit is open to communication. This could be movement just out of your vision, flashes of images in your mind, or a gentle touch or whisper.

4. If you sense the spirit is receptive, use your intuition to communicate with it, making your intention known. Return often to cultivate your relationship by leaving offerings, picking up trash, and otherwise caring for the land.

5. If you sense nothing, do not be deterred. Leave your offering and try again later.

CAYENNE HONEY COUGH SYRUP

No matter the season, persistent coughing and other throat issues abound. This syrup will help stifle that cough and soothe your throat and tonsil. It will also boost your immune system so you can get better faster. Apple cider vinegar, honey, and garlic are naturally antimicrobial, helping fight infections at the source. Honey also acts as a throat coat, soothing pain and swelling associated with coughing and tonsillitis. And cayenne pepper helps reduce inflammation.

Mason jar with lid

4 tablespoons apple
  cider vinegar

4 tablespoons local or
  raw honey

2 tablespoons water

½ teaspoon cayenne pepper

2 garlic cloves, minced

1. In the mason jar, combine all the ingredients and stir clockwise until well combined. As you stir, recite the following enchantment:

   "Mother Earth, I ask of thee,
   Bring health and protection to me.
   With pepper red and honey golden,
   This syrup shall mend all that is swollen.
   Help fight off this infection,
   Leaving the illness beyond detection."

2. Seal and store in refrigerator for up to a week. Take a spoonful as needed.

COURAGE TALISMAN

Talismans are magical objects designed to increase your power. This talisman will be unique to you and can be worn or carried on your person to boost your courage. Talismans can be made from a variety of materials. This talisman uses nettle, rosemary, or thyme—all associated with courage and strength. The sun also lends strength by infusing the talisman with power during the drying process. Create your talisman during the waxing or full moon.

2-inch ball of air-dry modeling clay
¼ teaspoon dried nettle, rosemary, and/or thyme
Small piece of wax paper
Toothpick (optional)

Crystal chips of your choosing—tiger's eye, aquamarine, or bloodstone (optional)
String or necklace chain (optional)

1. Work the modeling clay in your hands until thoroughly warmed and pliable. Add the herb(s) and work until well incorporated. As you do so, think about your intent behind making this talisman. Visualize yourself full of courage, overcoming obstacles, standing up for yourself and others, and setting firm boundaries.

2. Lay out the wax paper. Using your palm, flatten the clay onto it, forming a small disk or pendant.

3. Decorate the talisman as you desire. Use the toothpick to carve a design, symbol, or sigil you associate with courage, such as a lion, wolf, dagger, Uruz (rune), or Tiwaz (rune). Add crystal chips around the edges. If making into a necklace, pierce a hole in the top large enough to thread a chain or string through.

4. Place in the sun to charge and dry. Carry or wear to boost courage.

CREATIVITY-BOOSTING SPELL

Studies have shown that creative expression helps build resilience, grounds us in the present, and fosters empowerment. Just like meditation, creativity calms your mind and body. This spell will give you a creative boost, energizing you to keep building the skills you need to heal and engage in self-care. This simple spell uses a yellow candle and rosemary, which are both associated with creativity. Perform this spell whenever you need an extra boost in creativity. If you are focusing on a specific creative task, perform this spell and allow the candle to burn while you work.

Toothpick

Yellow candle

1 or 2 teaspoons dried rosemary

2 or 3 drops olive oil

Match or lighter

1. Using the toothpick, etch the word *creativity* into the candle or draw a light bulb, the symbol of creativity and new ideas.

2. Spread the rosemary out on a flat surface. Anoint the candle with a couple drops of olive oil and roll the candle through the ground rosemary until lightly covered.

CONTINUED

3. Light the candle and recite the following enchantment:

"Powers of air and fire bright,
Guide my hand in this creative rite.
Muses nine I summon thee,
Fill my mind with creativity.
Let inspiration fill my mind,
Leave all blockages behind.
Imagination grows within me,
As I will it, so shall it be."

4. Carefully hold your hands around the flame, being sure not to burn yourself. Feel the warmth of the flame and let it fill you with inspiration and creativity.

DANDELION DETOX TEA

Before I jump into this recipe, I want you to be abundantly aware of the deceptive practices of the modern wellness industry. Under the guise of health, corporations and influencers have worked hard to convince us that we need their costly products, fad diets, exercise plans, and procedures to remove deadly toxins from our bodies. Many of these claims are completely unsubstantiated—they are not supported by a single scientific study. Your body is naturally equipped to remove toxins from your body through your kidneys, liver, lungs, and even skin.

Most detoxing products are a sham, but there are things you can do to support your body's natural processes. This dandelion tea is a natural way to support your body's existing detoxification efforts. Dandelion root contains polysaccharides, which are known to reduce stress on the liver, support bile production, and aid your liver in the filtration process. It's also a natural diuretic, encouraging urination and reducing water retention, thus "flushing" your system, so to speak. Finally, dandelion is high in vitamin C, which acts as an antioxidant.

Heat-safe drinking vessel

1 cup boiling water

1 dandelion root tea bag

Honey, to taste

CONTINUED

1. In the drinking vessel, combine the water and dandelion root. Add the honey and stir clockwise while reciting the following enchantment:

    "Dandelion and honey combine,
    Help detox this body of mine.
    Flush my system and my liver reward,
    Warm my soul and leave me restored."

2. Hold your drinking vessel in both hands and visualize it filling with golden, healing light.

3. Drink up to three times a day followed by plenty of water.

SNAP OUT OF DISSOCIATION MANTRA

If you have mental illness or excessive stress, you may find yourself dissociating. Dissociation is a disconnection between you and the world around you and can include behaviors such as daydreaming, highway hypnosis, or even scrolling through social media for hours at a time. The most effective way to get out of a dissociative episode is to refocus on the present. This mantra, when combined with grounding techniques, will help snap you out of such an episode.

1. Take a deep breath through your nose for 4 seconds. Hold your breath for 7 seconds, then exhale completely through your mouth for 8 seconds. Repeat three times.

2. When calm, repeat the following mantra:

   "I am clear. I am present.
   I am alive. I exist in the now."

3. Repeat until you feel present in your reality. Follow up with grounding techniques, taking a walk outside, or eating a light snack.

EMOTIONAL HEALING WATER RITUAL

Harboring feelings of sadness, grief, guilt, anger, or other emotions associated with trauma can manifest physically as recurring illnesses. This ritual uses the healing energies of water to wash away those unwanted emotions. The flame works with the water to bring emotional well-being. The black, blue, and white candles represent your past, present, and future. Exercise caution when lighting candles outdoors. This spell can also be performed during a gentle rainstorm.

Running water, preferably from a natural source

Black, blue, and white candles
Match or lighter

1. Travel to your local water source or shower. Sit comfortably near the water and place your candles in front of you, black on the left, blue in the middle, and white on the right.

2. Light each candle while saying the following enchantment:

   "I let go of the past and heal my present self so that my future remains mine to choose. I forgive myself for my past mistakes and chose happiness. I start over with a clean slate."

3. Place your hands or entire body in the running water and close your eyes. Visualize yourself releasing your unwanted emotions and the water carrying them away. Feel the water calming your mind and filling you with healing energies. Hold this visualization for as long as you need. You may feel the desire to hell, scream, or cry. Do so.

4. When finished, extinguish the candles and say:

   "I am restored. So I will it, so shall it be."

SPELL BAG FOR EMPOWERMENT

At every turn, we are faced with obstacles seeking to strip us of our confidence, strength, and even basic rights. Empowerment is the process of becoming stronger and learning to take control of your life. This spell incorporates the Chariot, the card of empowerment, triumph, achievement, and overcoming obstacles. The card is combined with red pepper flakes and cinnamon for strength, cloves for protection, black salt to remove blockages, and clear quartz to amplify your power. Carry the spell bag on you for interviews, presentations, speeches, or protests to ensure your success and protect you from harm. Create this spell during the full moon.

Red or black spell bag
The Chariot tarot card, printed
  small enough to fit into
  spell bag
1 or 2 teaspoons red
  pepper flakes

1 cinnamon stick
1 or 2 teaspoons whole cloves
1 or 2 teaspoons black salt
Clear quartz crystal

1. Cleanse the spell bag using your preferred cleansing method.

2. Hold the Chariot card in your hand, visualizing it filling you with strength and confidence as it warms. Place it in your spell bag.

3. Next add the spices and quartz, visualizing your intent as you do so.

CONTINUED

4. Tie the spell bag shut, hold it in both hands, and recite the following enchantment:

"Remove the barriers that stand in my way. Bring me the strength and confidence to control my destiny. Help me fight against those who would oppress me. So I will it, so shall it be."

5. Blow your intention into the spell bag. Carry the bag on your person to empower you.

ENERGY-BOOSTING TEA

Feeling run-down, tired, or sluggish? Same, but this energy-boosting tea will leave you feeling alert and energized in no time. However, if you are constantly feeling run-down, tired, or sluggish, this could be a sign of a larger issue, and I encourage you to seek medical attention. A good night's rest is better than a shot of caffeine. With that said, yerba mate is an herbal tea rich in xanthines, which act as stimulants to wake you up. It also contains saponins and polyphenols, which are antioxidants that reduce stress, lower cholesterol, and fight disease. Combined with peppermint, which is naturally stimulating, these ingredients create a powerful energy booster to help you get through the day. Drink first thing in the morning.

Drinking vessel

1 cup hot (175°F/80°C) water

2 teaspoons dried yerba mate

1 teaspoon dried peppermint

Sweetener, to taste

Tea ball or strainer

1. In the drinking vessel, combine the hot water, yerba mate, and peppermint. Cover and brew for 5 minutes. Strain the herbs or remove tea ball and compost the remains.

2. Add your sweetener of choice, stirring clockwise to draw energy toward you. As you do so, recite the following enchantment:

   "Drive away fatigue and awaken my senses,
   Leave me feeling alert and refreshed."

3. Visualize the tea filling with energetic orange light.

4. Enjoy, feeling the tea's energy pouring into you, leaving you feeling awake and alert.

UPLIFTING ROOM SPRAY

Sometimes the energy in our home can feel stagnant or heavy, even after a thorough cleansing. This room spray is designed to revitalize the space, uplift the energy, and bring peace and harmony back to your home. Chamomile is associated with relaxation and happiness, and rose brings loving, nurturing energies into the space. This spray also uses rosemary to promote clarity of mind, and citrine which is magically associated with energy, happiness, and joy. Create this uplifting room spray during the full or waxing moon to draw happiness and peace to you.

4-ounce spray bottle

4 tablespoons distilled water

2 tablespoons witch hazel
 or vodka

20 drops chamomile
 essential oil*

10 drops rose essential oil*

1 rosemary sprig

Citrine crystal, small enough to
 fit into the bottle

1. In the spray bottle, combine all the ingredients and gently shake while reciting the following enchantment:

   "Calming chamomile and loving rose,
   Sprig of rosemary and golden citrine.
   Banish all negativity and bring repose,
   Uplift the energies and make it serene. "

2. Spray freely around your space, visualizing the energies in your space rising.

*You can substitute 30 to 40 drops of any uplifting essential oils in this recipe, such as grapefruit, lemongrass, rosemary, or lavender, and change the wording of the incantation accordingly. Keep in mind that grapefruit, lemongrass, and rosemary essential oils are toxic to cats.

EXERCISE   CATEGORY: BODY

MINDFUL MOVEMENT

Moving your body is extremely important to maintaining overall health, as it stimulates blood flow, reduces inflammation, and strengthens your heart. However, not all movement needs to be strenuous to be beneficial. Engaging in mindful movements helps you reap the rewards of exercise while also reducing stress, strengthening your mind and body connection, and releasing unwanted, stagnant energy. These movements and stretches are low impact and can be modified or enhanced. If your mobility limits the type of stretching you can do, focus on breathing and feel free to modify any stretches to meet your physical needs.

1. Begin by standing or sitting comfortably.

2. Take a deep breath through your nose for 4 seconds. Hold your breath for 7 seconds, then exhale completely through your mouth for 8 seconds. Repeat three times.

3. Once relaxed, stand (or sit) with your feet hip-width apart. Inhale and reach both arms forward. Interlock your fingers, palms facing outward, and reach overhead, arching your spine. Exhale and hold for 5 to 10 seconds. Repeat.

4. With your hands still interlocked, inhale and reach your arms overhead. Lean to the right and exhale. Hold for 5 to 10 seconds. Repeat on the left side.

5. Lower your arms and interlock your hands in front of your chest, forming a fist. Inhale and twist your spine left and right. Exhale and hold each stretch for 3 seconds.

CONTINUED

6. Let your arms fall to your sides and slowly roll your neck forward and around for 10 seconds.

7. Next, roll your shoulders forward ten times and back ten times.

8. End by going for a walk, dancing in your seat, or marching in place for 1 to 5 minutes, followed by drinking plenty of water.

BANISHING FEAR SPELL

Fear often stands in the way of our own self-progress, whether it be the fear of rejection, failure, or even something small like a wasp. Yeah, that last one is definitely me. This simple spell will help trap and banish your fear, preventing it from getting in your way. There are two options for this spell: you can use a houseplant or black tourmaline or onyx to soak up your fear. Plants, black tourmaline, and onyx are great at soaking up unwanted energies and banishing them, making them the perfect receptacle for what you wish to rid yourself of.

4-by-4-inch piece of paper   **Candle**
Writing utensil   **Match or lighter**
Houseplant or black tourmaline/
  black onyx crystal

1. Along the four sides of the paper, write *I am fearless,* creating a box.

2. In the center, write your fear, being as clear and concise as possible. As you do so say the following enchantment:

    "I confine my fear to this box,
    And demand its hold over me stop.
    You are no longer welcome here,
    It is time you disappear."

3. Fold the paper away from you twice and place it under the plant or crystal. Visualize the plant or crystal soaking up your fear. Leave overnight.

4. The following day, remove the paper from under the plant or crystal. Light the candle and burn the piece of paper, visualizing the connection between you and your fear being completely broken.

GROW WITH ME
SPELL FOR FRIENDSHIP

Having a solid group of friends, no matter how small, increases your overall happiness and wellness. This spell will help you cultivate a friendship, whether old or new, using a plant to symbolize the relationship. Remember, relationships take work, as does caring for a plant. In order for this spell to work, you will need to dedicate time to both your plant and your relationship on a weekly basis. If the plant shows signs of disease or dies, it may indicate a problem in your friendship. Care for both to ensure a lasting friendship—that is, unless the friendship no longer serves you. Remember that sometimes, it's okay to let people go.

Pot	Moss agate crystal
Potting soil, to fill	Amethyst crystal
Basil, lavender, mint, or	Rose quartz crystal
coleus seeds	Mister or spray bottle with water

1. Begin by cleansing the pot using your preferred cleansing method.

2. Fill the pot with potting soil. On the top of the soil, use your finger to write the full name of your friend.

3. Hold the seed(s) in both of your hands and gently whisper the following enchantment:

   *"As this seed grows so shall my friendship
   with [insert name here].
   It blossoms and strengthens each day.
   So I will it, so it shall be."*

4. Plant the seed according to the package directions.

5. Place the moss agate, amethyst, and rose quartz in a circle around the seed you planted and say the following enchantment:

   "With moss agate to balance, amethyst for health, and rose quartz for love and compassion, I bless this friendship."

6. Water the seeds according to their needs. Mist lightly daily, repeating the enchantment in step 3.

GRATITUDE JOURNALING

We often forget the amazing healing powers of showing grat-
itude. A 2008 study found that showing gratitude lights up
the reward pathways in your brain, boosting serotonin and
dopamine, the chemicals associated with memory and pleasure.
In short, showing gratitude increases happiness, reduces stress,
and boosts memory. Now that isn't to say this is a cure-all or
that you should always be positive. Quite the contrary. I am a
huge supporter of being negative, but sometimes, we need to let
that negativity go and be thankful for how much we have.

Notebook or journal   **White, pink, or light blue candle**
Writing utensil   **Match or lighter**

1. Begin by sitting in a comfortable position with your notebook or journal and writing utensil in front of you.

2. Take a deep breath through your nose for 4 seconds. Hold your breath for 7 seconds, then exhale completely through your mouth for 8 seconds. Repeat until relaxed.

3. When ready, light the candle and begin journaling on the following prompts:

   ◆ What is the best thing that happened today?

   ◆ What is something you are proud of in your personal or pro-fessional life?

   ◆ Describe one thing that has changed your life for the better and why.

   ◆ Describe what you love most about yourself and why.

   ◆ Make a list of at least twenty-five things you are grateful for.

4. When finished, read through your answers, feeling gratitude overwhelm you.

5. Finish this exercise by saying:

   "I am grateful."

6. Snuff out your candle.

GROUNDING
ROOT VEGETABLE STEW

Connecting with the earth through food is a fantastic way to ground, reduce stress, and otherwise reset to promote health and wellness. Root vegetables and mushrooms are naturally grounding foods, and thyme and rosemary help uplift your energies and refocus your mind.

Medium skillet
1 yellow onion, chopped
4 garlic cloves, minced
Slow cooker
1 rutabaga, peeled and cubed
3 carrots, peeled and sliced
5 Yukon Gold potatoes, cubed
½ pound button
   mushrooms, sliced
2 tablespoons tomato paste

2 fresh rosemary sprigs
1 thyme sprig
1 bay leaf
½ teaspoon onion powder
½ teaspoon garlic powder
Salt
Freshly ground black pepper
3 cups vegetable stock
1 teaspoon olive oil
Blender

1. In a medium skillet, sauté the onions until they are translucent. Add the garlic and cook until fragrant, about 1 minute.

2. Add the onions and garlic to the slow cooker, along with the rest of the ingredients. Stir clockwise until well combined.

3. Cook on high for 3 or 4 hours or on low for 5 or 6 hours.

4. Remove the rosemary, thyme, and bay leaf. Pour 1 cup of the stew into the blender and blend until smooth. Add the puree back to the stew and stir clockwise while saying the following enchantment:

> *"Roots of earth and herbs of plenty,*
> *Ground and center my soulful energies.*
> *Realign what is amiss,*
> *And bring me back into bliss.*
> *So I will it, so it is."*

5. Ladle the stew into a bowl and breathe in the aroma, feeling its warmth travel through you. Enjoy!

GUT-HEALING BROTH

Your gut microbiome plays a key role in your overall health. Research, including that of Dawson, Dash, and Jacka published in the International Review of Neurobiology, *has drawn a link between gut health and physical as well as mental well-being. This vegan-friendly broth combines vitamin-packed, gut-friendly vegetables, herbs, and spices to nourish your body, stave off illness, and promote general wellness. It also involves the Uruz (rune), which is associated with healing and strength. Feel free to adjust the recipe to include ingredients that are culturally significant to you, such as miso or sustainably sourced palm oil.*

Large pot

12 cups filtered water

1 tablespoon extra-virgin olive oil

1 cup shiitake or cremini
mushrooms

1 whole red onion,
coarsely chopped

1 garlic head, cloves smashed

2 cups coarsely chopped kale

½ cup kombu or nori seaweed

3 carrots, coarsely chopped

3 celery stalks,
coarsely chopped

1 parsley bunch

2 fresh rosemary sprigs

5 fresh sage leaves

2 bay leaves

1-inch piece fresh ginger root,
coarsely chopped

2 tablespoons ground turmeric

1 tablespoon black peppercorns

1 tablespoon tamari

1 jalapeño, coarsely chopped
(optional)

1. In a large pot, combine all the ingredients. Bring to a boil, then lower the heat to a simmer.

2. Using a spoon, trace the Uruz (rune) into the broth mixture while reciting the following enchantment:

   "By air, earth, fire, and water, nourish my body and heal what ails me."

3. Cover and simmer for 2 hours, stirring clockwise occasionally.

4. Strain liquid through a fine-mesh strainer and discard the plant matter in your compost.

5. Enjoy immediately or store in glass jars in the refrigerator for up to 1 week.

HAPPY HOME SPELL JAR

Though it may sometimes seem out of reach, we truly can create our own happiness. This spell jar will help you harness happiness in the home by reducing stress and promoting love, happiness, and luck. It contains lavender for peace, lemon and citrine for happiness, basil and roses for love, thyme for balance, sesame for prosperity, cinnamon for wealth, cloves for growth, and honey to sweeten the deal. The bottle is charged with sunlight to strengthen its powers. Create this jar during the waxing or full moon.

Small bottle with stopper or lid
1 part dried lavender
1 part dried lemon peel
1 part dried basil
1 part dried thyme
1 part sesame seeds
1 part ground cinnamon
1 part ground cloves

1 part dried rose petals
2 drops honey
Citrine crystal (small enough to fit into bottle)
Matches or lighter
Yellow candle
Toothpick
The Sun tarot card (optional)

1. Begin by cleansing your bottle using your preferred cleansing method.

2. Layer each of the ingredients, lavender through honey, while visualizing your home filled with happiness, love, and abundance.

3. Hold the citrine in your hand and recite the following enchantment:

   *"Citrine yellow and bright,
   Bring happiness and delight."*

4. Place the citrine it in the bottle and seal. Light the yellow candle and drip wax around the lid or cork until completely sealed. Use a toothpick to carve a Wunjo (rune) in the wax to harmonize energies.

5. Charge in full sunlight or on the Sun tarot card for 12 hours.

6. Place in a prominent location in your home where you will see it daily.

HEADACHE RELIEF ESSENTIAL OIL BLEND

As a chronic headache sufferer, I have found a number of ways to treat the pain without over-the-counter medications, which can put unnecessary strain on your kidneys and liver if taken in excess. Essential oils may mitigate tension and stress-related headaches. Rosemary, eucalyptus, lavender, and peppermint essential oils are naturally calming and cooling. These essential oils also stimulate blood flow, opening blood vessels and relieving tension-related pain. Amethyst, which is magically associated with tension and stress relief, enhances the healing properties of the oil blend. Create this blend during the waning moon, which is associated with pain removal and banishment.

10-ml brown rollerball bottle or glass bottle with cap
2 drops peppermint essential oil*
2 drops rosemary essential oil*
2 drops eucalyptus essential oil*
2 drops lavender essential oil*

1 or 2 amethyst crystal chips, small enough to fit into the bottle
Carrier oil, such as fractionated coconut oil, to fill

1. In the bottle, combine the essential oils and amethyst chips and cover with the carrier oil.

2. Gently roll the bottle between the palms of your hands while saying the following enchantment:

   "May the scent of herbs relieve my tension.
   May the touch of amethyst draw out my pain.
   Combined, leave your healing energy behind.
   As I will it, so it is."

3. Gently apply the oil to your temples, visualizing the pain being pulled away from you.

*If you don't have access to essential oils, you can create a tea blend using 1 teaspoon of dried peppermint and lavender, ½ teaspoon dried rosemary, and 2 teaspoons black tea. Brew in boiling water for 5 minutes. Sweeten if desired.

HEALING HYDRATION RITUAL

Staying hydrated is a great way to maintain overall health and connect with the element water daily. Drinking enough water helps regulate body temperature, cushion your joints, flush waste, promote memory, stave off hunger, and even elevate your mood. Perform this ritual in the morning to wake up your body, ready your digestive system for food, and amplify your connection with the natural element water.

Glass of cool water

Amethyst or other water-safe crystal*, thoroughly washed (optional)

1. Begin by grounding and centering, making sure your mind, body, and spirit are focused on the present moment.

2. If using, place the amethyst in your water, visualizing it filling the water with nourishing energies.

3. Hold the glass of water in your hand(s) and close your eyes. Begin lightly meditating on the healing properties of water, envisioning it washing away your fatigue, aches, pains, and negative feelings and emotions.

4. Open your eyes and say,

> *"Spirit of water, wild and free,*
> *Flow through to hydrate me.*
> *Awaken my body and nourish my mind,*
> *Gift me with your healing kind.*
> *Wash away all weariness,*
> *Leave me feeling completely refreshed."*

5. Drink the water, being mindful not to swallow the crystal. Feel its energy flowing through you, awakening your body and readying you for the day.

*Feel free to switch the amethyst out with another nontoxic, water-safe crystal to boost your intention, such as tiger's eye for strength or smoky quartz for cleansing.

INTRUSIVE THOUGHTS BEGONE SPELL

Despite our best efforts, intrusive thoughts can still manage to plague us. You could perform every spell and ritual in this book and yet still find yourself plagued by self-doubt, violent thoughts, worries, or reminders of past traumatic events. Use this quick spell to get release those thoughts. Sometimes writing them down and casting them out is the best way to get rid of them.

Sheet of paper   **Black or white candle (optional)**
Writing utensil   **Match or lighter (optional)**

1. On a sheet of paper, write down your intrusive thought. Limit this to one thought per sheet of paper. (If you are plagued by many, repeat this ritual for each thought.)

2. Fold the paper away from you twice and draw a sigil or symbol you associate with banishment, halting, or binding (such as the stop symbol, a circle with line through it).

3. Dispose of the paper using your preferred elemental method. For example, you can burn the paper, flush it down the toilet, rip it up and throw it into the wind, or bury it in the earth. As you do so, visualize the intrusive thought leaving you and recite the following enchantment:

   "I banish my intrusive thought of [insert thought here]. You will no longer bother me. Leave me now and never return. So I will it, so it shall be."

4. If possible, complete the spell by bathing, and wash with an uplifting-smelling soap.

SCALES OF JUSTICE RITUAL

Witchcraft has long been used as a means of righting wrongs. For many, it has been one of the only ways to fight back against oppressors. Use this spell to seek justice for yourself or others by bringing an oppressor's crimes to light.

Mortar and pestle
1 teaspoon dried calendula
1 teaspoon dried oregano
1 teaspoon dried celandine
1 teaspoon dried basil
Charcoal disk

Fire-safe dish
Match or lighter
Justice tarot card
Small animal bone or plastic
　bone buried in a bowl of sand

1. In the mortar and pestle, blend the herbs until they form a well-combined fine powder.

2. Light the charcoal in the dish and, when the charcoal is completely ashy gray, add the herbal incense blend.

3. Place the Justice tarot card in front of the incense. Put the bowl of sand and bone on top of the card.

4. Place your hands over the top of the bowl and say the following incantation:

> *"I call out for justice to make things right,*
> *Although it lies buried, it shall be brought to light.*
> *[insert name(s)], though you hide your misdeeds,*
> *Thinking power and station protect your needs,*
> *All eyes are upon you and see through your deception,*
> *I reveal your injustices without exception.*
> *You are called to answer for your crimes,*
> *Stand now for you are out of time."*

CONTINUED

5. Shake the bowl back and forth to reveal the bone, visualizing the person being held accountable for their actions.

6. Repeat for each offender or victim or until your intuition tells you the spell is complete.

LUCK IN LOVE OIL BLEND

Studies have shown that stable, healthy, loving relationships have a number of concrete health benefits. They can reduce anxiety, lower blood pressure, increase natural healing, boost memory, and increase your overall life span by strengthening your immune system. This oil blend will help you have better luck with love, whether you are looking for a new partner or strengthening an existing relationship. Jasmine is a natural aphrodisiac and mood booster associated with love, passion, and friendship. Frankincense reduces stress, making you more open to new opportunities. Sweet orange boosts confidence and natural charm. Together, they create a potent, relationship-attracting blend. If you are mindful about when you craft it, you can infuse this blend with a particular energy depending on the relationship you wish to draw you to you. Fridays are associated with love, relationships, and attraction whereas Mondays are associated with confidence, vitality, charisma and hope. Create this blend during the waxing moon, preferably on Friday or Monday.

10-ml roller bottle or bottle with lid

4 drops jasmine essential oil*

3 drops frankincense essential oil*

3 drops sweet orange essential oil*

Rose quartz crystal chip, small enough to fit in the bottle

Carrier oil, such as rose hip oil, to fill the bottle

CONTINUED

1. In the roller bottle, combine the essential oils and crystal and top with your carrier oil of choice. Seal the bottle.

2. Gently roll the bottle between your hands while visualizing the oil blend filling with bright pink light, the color of love and friendship.

3. Apply to your wrists, behind your ears, or on your collarbone to attract love and friendship.

   *If you don't have access to essential oils, you can use dried herbs instead. See the note on Self-Confidence Essential Oil Blend (page 78) for more details.

GOOD LUCK SPELL JAR

Need to turn the tides in your favor? Use this good luck spell jar if you have run into a string of bad luck, need help securing a new job or relationship, or are worried about doing well on a test or event. White rice, oregano, and jade are associated with good luck, and basil, mint, and the color green are associated with prosperity, wealth, and abundance. Perform this spell during the waxing moon, preferably on a Thursday, the day associated with wealth and prosperity.

Small jar or vial with lid
  or stopper
1 part white rice
1 part oregano
1 part basil
1 part chamomile

1 part mint
Jade or citrine crystal chips,
  small enough to fit into the jar
Green candle
Match or lighter
Toothpick

1. Cleanse your spell jar using your preferred cleansing method.

2. Layer the ingredients—the rice through the jade/citrine crystal, holding your intention firmly in your mind. Seal the jar.

3. Light the green candle and drip wax around lid or stopper. As you do so, say the following enchantment:

   "Health, wealth, and luck abound,
   Come to me and surround.
   I attract all that I desire,
   I have all that I require."

4. When the wax dries, use the toothpick to carve the symbol of Jupiter, ♃, in the wax.

5. Carry on your person or place in a prominent location in your home to bring good luck and fortune to you.

MOTIVATING MINTY MATCHA SMOOTHIE

It can be extremely difficult to stay motivated. Motivation is especially hard to muster if you are overworked, overtired, or have depression or anxiety. This is completely normal. In fact, you shouldn't be going through life believing you have to be productive all the time. That type of capitalist thinking is designed to keep you oppressed. However, during the times when you want or need to remain motivated, and this smoothie is there to help. Bananas, pineapple, and chia seeds boost your mood; avocado and hemp seeds lessen anxiety; spinach improves memory; matcha improves attention and stimulates the mind; and mint increases blood flow to the brain and reduces mental fatigue. Combined, they create a potent witch's brew sure to keep you motivated (and full) for hours. I encourage you to drink this smoothie not just for work, but for personal pleasure as well.

Blender
½ frozen banana
¼ to ½ avocado
½ cup frozen pineapple
1 handful baby spinach
1 or 2 teaspoons matcha powder
1 cup oat milk

1 tablespoon chia or hemp seeds
½ cup fresh mint or 1 or 2 drops
   peppermint extract
Honey or maple syrup, to taste

1. In the blender, combine all the ingredients except the honey and blend until smooth.

2. Add the honey and stir clockwise while saying the following enchantment:

   "Bring me encouragement to complete my tasks,
   I am filled with motivation at last.
   Awaken the strength in my heart,
   To accomplish the mission on which I embark."

3. Consume while visualizing yourself full of motivation and completing whatever you set your mind to.

OUT WITH THE OLD, IN WITH THE NEW JOB SPELL

Finding a new job can be difficult and even a little scary. But if your current one is not serving your highest needs, it's time to make a change. If you are struggling to break away from a toxic job environment, remember that you are not required to stay at a job out of some perceived loyalty. Toxic job environments can take a serious toll on your health, increasing stress, anxiety, depression, and fatigue. This spell will help you break ties with your current job while simultaneously helping you find a better one. You may want to personalize the verbal statements in this spell based on your situation. Focus on your intentions and what you visualize for yourself.

Toothpick

Black candle

White candle

1 teaspoon ground
   cayenne pepper

1 teaspoon ground black pepper

½ teaspoon olive oil

1 teaspoon ground cinnamon

1 teaspoon ground rosemary

Match or lighter

1. Using the toothpick, write your current job on the black candle. On the white candle write *New job that better serves me.*

2. Mix the cayenne and black pepper. Anoint the black candle with half the oil and roll it in the herbs. Place to your left.

3. Mix the cinnamon and rosemary. Anoint the white candle with half the oil and roll it in the herbs. Place to your right.

4. Light the black candle and say:

"My job no longer serves me. The pay is too little, the stress too high, and the environment too toxic. I have the strength to quit and find something new."

5. Visualize standing up for yourself and quitting the job.

6. Next, light the white candle and say:

"I have a new job that better serves me. The pay is high, the stress is low, and the environment is friendly. My life is full of abundance."

7. Visualize yourself happy at your new job.

8. Allow both candles to burn out completely.

ORGANIZATION MANTRA AND TALISMAN

Getting and staying organized can be difficult, especially if you are neurodivergent like me. However, an organized environment can have a profoundly positive impact on your mental, emotional, and physical well-being. Living in a disorganized space can negatively impact our thoughts and emotions, contributing to stress and illness. This mantra and clear quartz talisman will help put you into the right mindset and hype you up to organize. Clear quartz is associated with removing blockages and amplifying energy, and will help you stay focused on the organizing task at hand. Start small and keep in mind that organization looks different for everyone; what works for one person may not work for you. Your home is not going to look like a spread in **Better Homes & Gardens** *or be Pinterest-perfect all the time. Accepting this and finding joy in your own space is one of the first steps toward true self-care and healing.*

Clear quartz crystal   **Uplifting music**

1. Sit or stand in a comfortable position.

2. Hold the clear quartz in both hands and repeat the following mantra three times:

   "I am capable. I am focused.
   Organization comes easily to me.
   My space is organized and clear.
   So I will it, so shall it be."

3. Place the quartz in your pocket and touch each time you feel yourself getting distracted from the task at hand. Repeat the mantra if needed.

4. Turn on some uplifting music and start organizing!

LET ITEMS GO SPELL

When it comes to healing old wounds and moving forward, letting go of items with negative associations is key. Some items simply connect us back to our trauma or leave us feeling cluttered and confined. These could be old photographs, clothing, books, gifts, or broken items. This simple spell is designed to help you let go of these items and break the threads connecting you to your past traumas. Remember to start small; this isn't a race.

Pendulum
Sheet of paper
Writing utensil

Match or lighter
Black or white candle

1. Begin by picking an area you wish to organize and declutter.

2. Starting on the right side of the space and working left, pick up the first item you see. Hold it in your hands and feel its energy. Does this item still serve you? If it doesn't, hug it, thank it for its service, and put it in a pile to trash, donate, or give away. If it does, place it in the keep pile.

3. If you come across an item that you are unsure of, use your pendulum to help you decide. When you have determined your pendulum's *yes* and *no,* hold the pendulum above the item to see what it suggests.

4. When you have finished clearing the space, clean the area thoroughly and put the items you are keeping back in their spots.

5. On a sheet of paper, list the items you are getting rid of. Light the candle and burn the paper, thus severing all connections you have with the items. Promptly remove them from your home.

AILMENT BANISHING RITUAL

Often when we have a physical, mental, or spiritual ailment, it appears in our mind's eye as an oily green or sticky black ooze. This ooze can be removed using many different techniques, including energy cleansing, repairing teas, and detoxing baths. My favorite method of removal, however, is through creative imagery and physical movement. This method will not cure a serious illness, but it can help alleviate pain and stress. When we visualize pulling that sticky ooze out of our body, we can trick the brain into believing the cause of the ailment is gone. The body and mind are two sides of the same coin. This exercise is especially effective for metaphysical ailments, but if the ailment is purely physical, be sure to follow up with medical treatment if needed.

1. Begin by standing, sitting, or lying comfortably in a quiet place where you will not be disturbed.

2. Close your eyes and visualize yourself as you are.

3. Scan your body in your mind's eye, looking for the source of your problem.

4. When you find it, grab it with your hands and pull it from your body. Visualize it being removed completely. You may feel tension or the desire to gag or retch as you pull. This is natural.

5. Continue this visualization and removal until all the "ooze" is gone.

6. End this ritual by eating a light snack and drinking a cool glass of water.

BODILY MAINTENANCE MEDITATION

Knowing thyself is a key tenet of witchcraft and plays an important role in healing and self-care. Sometimes we know something is wrong without really knowing what exactly. This meditation is designed to help you get in touch with your physical self. When we familiarize ourselves with our physical presence, it helps establish a baseline with which to gauge our health. As we age, however, this baseline will change, so it's important to engage in this meditation regularly.

Match or lighter
Rosemary incense
Incense tray
White candle
Labradorite (or tiger's
  eye) crystal

Blue lace agate (or
  amethyst) crystal
Writing utensil
Notebook or journal

1. Begin by standing, sitting, or lying comfortably in a quiet place where you will not be disturbed for 20 to 30 minutes.

2. Light the rosemary incense and candle and say:

    "Burn away the fog and bring me wisdom and clarity."

3. Place the crystals in front of you or hold them in your hands and say:

    "Bring me self-awareness so I may know myself better."

4. Close your eyes and bring your awareness into your body, starting with your toes or the lowest point you are able. Flex and stretch them back, taking note of what feels good, bad, or neutral. When ready, move on to your feet, then legs, stomach, etc., spending 1 to 3 minutes on each bodily region.

5. When finished, open your eyes and take a deep breath. Thank your body for all it provides and record your insights in your notebook or journal while the candle and incense burn out.

6. Afterward, eat a light snack and drink a cool glass of water to ground and rehydrate.

FIRE CIDER FOR COLD AND FLU

Fire cider is an herbal folk remedy used to boost the immune system and stave off illness. The recipe can change based on what's available, but it generally contains vinegar, onion, garlic, peppers, citrus, and spices. It can be taken by the spoonful, added to soups and salads, or mixed into sautéed vegetables.

1-quart mason jar with lid

1 red onion, chopped

10 garlic cloves, minced

2 jalapeño or habanero peppers, chopped

Juice and grated zest of 1 lemon

1-inch piece fresh ginger root, peeled and chopped

1-inch piece horseradish root, peeled and chopped

1 tablespoon ground turmeric

2 tablespoons fresh rosemary (or 1 teaspoon dried rosemary)

1 teaspoon black peppercorns

Raw apple cider vinegar, to cover

Parchment paper

Cheesecloth

¼ cup local honey

Matches or lighter

Red candle

Knife or carving tool

1. In the mason jar, combine the vegetables and cover them with the vinegar.

2. Place the parchment paper on top of the mason jar and seal.

3. Shake the jar vigorously, visualizing it filling with fiery red light.

4. Store in a cool, dark place, shaking daily for 1 month while repeating the visualization.

5. Using the cheesecloth, strain out the pulp over a bowl. Squeeze to remove all of the liquid.

6. Add honey and stir clockwise until incorporated. Pour the mixture back into the mason jar and seal.

7. Light the red candle and say the following enchantment:

"Fire hot and fire bright,
Burn away all illness on sight."

8. Drip a couple of drops of red wax on top of the jar lid. When dry, carve a Kenaz (rune) (inner fire and heat) into the wax.

9. Store in a cool, dark place for up to a year.

BLACK CAT ANOINTING OIL FOR PROTECTION AND CURSE REMOVAL

Black cats have long been associated with witchcraft. Many people believe black cats bring bad luck, but the exact opposite is true. Black is associated with banishment, binding, protection, and curse breaking. To create a potent protection charm, you can use the hair and whiskers of a black cat. Never pull hair or whiskers from a cat—instead, use what they naturally shed. This oil combines the protective and banishing powers of the black cat with that of cedar, cinnamon, and frankincense.

6-ounce mason jar

½ cup olive oil

15 to 20 drops cedar essential oil or 2 tablespoons dried cedar

10 drops cinnamon essential oil or 1 tablespoon ground cinnamon

10 drops frankincense essential oil or 1 tablespoon frankincense resin

1 naturally shed black cat hair or whisker

Black onyx crystal (optional)

1. In the mason jar, combine the olive oil and essential oils. Stir counterclockwise while saying the following enchantment:

   "With essence of earth a spell I cast,
   A ward of protection to hold me fast.
   Be a shield around me and behind,
   Any curses or hexes it shall bind.
   No ill will may come my way,
   I am protected night and day."

2. Add the cat hair or whisker and black onyx (if using) and say the following enchantment:

   "Feline spirit black as night I call to thee, to request your aid. Bring me good luck, protect me from evil, and keep me and mine safe."

3. Use this oil to anoint candles, windows, doors, or yourself to aid in protection spells and rituals, or to remove a curse, hex, or evil eye. Repeat the enchantments while applying the oil.

DECOY POPPET

Poppets are small doll-like items that are commonly used for protection. A poppet acts as a sympathetic representation of a person, designed to take the brunt of any baneful magic, ill will, or bad luck. The poppet is tied to its owner through a DNA tag, such as nail clippings, hair, saliva, or even blood. Poppets, like all protection magic, must be routinely recharged and fed. This can be done by refreshing the poppet's salt and offering it herbs, crystals, or coins. If you ever feel the need to replace the poppet, thank it for its service and bury it. To protect yourself from harm, create this poppet and let it redirect any negativity that is headed your way.

2 (6-inch) squares of biodegradable fabric in your favorite color
Writing utensil
Scissors
Sewing needle
Black thread

Doll stuffing
Hematite crystal
A bit of your hair, nails, saliva, or blood
½ cup salt
Mason jar

1. On the back of each piece of fabric, draw the outline of a human. Cut out your shape.

2. Keeping the back of the fabric facing out, sew the two pieces of fabric together around the edges of the poppet, leaving an opening at the head.

3. Turn the fabric right-side out and place some stuffing in the feet and body.

4. Hold the hematite in your hand until warm while visualizing it filling with protective energies. Place the hematite and DNA tag in your poppet.

5. Fill the rest of the way with stuffing and sew shut.

6. Hug the poppet and say:

"Poppet of mine, keep me safe. Redirect all negativity, ill will, and bad luck away from me."

7. Pour the salt into the bottom of the mason jar.

8. Kiss the poppet and place it in the mason jar.

9. Place the mason jar somewhere inconspicuous. Recharge once a month.

PROTECTION FLOOR WASH

Magical floor washes have been used in folk magic for centuries to protect and cleanse homes. This recipe combines the protective and cleansing properties of rosemary, basil, mint, and bay with the banishing qualities of white vinegar and salt to create a potent protective barrier around your home. Some of these ingredients also act as an insect repellant, keeping your home free of unwanted pests. This wash can also be used on walls, doors, and window frames. If applying everywhere, work from top to bottom, cleaning your floors last.

Pot with lid

2 tablespoons fresh rosemary (or
  1 teaspoon dried rosemary)

¼ cup chopped fresh basil or
  2 tablespoons dried basil

¼ cup chopped fresh mint or
  2 tablespoons dried mint

2 bay leaves

8 cups boiling water

Cheesecloth

Mop bucket

2 cups vinegar

¼ cup salt

Mop

1. In the pot, combine the herbs with the boiling water and cover. Steep for 10 minutes.

2. Using the cheesecloth, strain the infusion into the mop bucket. Compost the plant material that has been strained out.

3. Add the vinegar and salt, then stir the mixture clockwise while visualizing it filling with protective light.

4. Mop your floors with the mixture, starting at the back of the home and working your way toward the front door. As you mop, visualize a protective barrier forming around your home.

5. When finished, flush the use mop water down the toilet, visualizing any unwanted energies being washed away with it.

WITCH'S LADDER FOR PEACE AND PROTECTION

The witch's ladder is a traditional protection charm made from knotted cords, feathers, and charms. This one incorporates bells, which have historically been used to protect a space and alert those within a space about a visitor. It will bring protection, peace, and clear communication.

Black yarn or thread
9 small silver bells
Blue yarn or thread

Yellow yarn or thread
Rosemary or sage essential oil
Pentacle charm (optional)

1. Starting with the black yarn or thread, tie a loop large enough to slip onto your door handle. Thread your first bell through the black thread.

2. Begin braiding or plaiting the blue and yellow yarn with the black while chanting.

   "Black for protection; blue for peace; yellow for communication; I create this charm. I weave my intent into these knots."

3. When you have woven 2 or 3 inches, tie in another bell using the black yarn or thread.

4. Repeat steps 2 and 3 until all the bells are attached.

5. Weave 1 or 2 inches more, repeating the enchantment. Attach the pentacle charm, if using, or tie a knot while saying:

   "In this home, we are protected, peaceful, and communicate openly. So it is."

6. Anoint each of the bell knots with rosemary or sage essential oil and hang the ladder on your front door.

CORD-CUTTING RITUAL TO END A TOXIC RELATIONSHIP

When we form a relationship with someone, it results in energetic ties that link us together. These ties can result from a relationship with a partner, family, job, or even an object. Sometimes these relationships build us up, support us, and provide us with a boost. Other times, these relationships tear us down, sucking the life out of us. You may not be able to completely end a relationship or quit your job, but you can cut energetic ties and shield yourself from further energy drain. I have found that once this happens, the universe often presents us with better opportunities. Perform this spell during the waning or dark moon.

**Scissors, athame, or
 obsidian blade**

1. Sit or stand comfortably somewhere you will not be disturbed.

2. Take a deep breath through your nose for four seconds. Hold your breath for seven seconds, then exhale completely through your mouth for eight seconds.

3. Close your eyes and visualize the relationship you wish to cut ties with. See the threads that link you together.

4. When you have a firm visualization of your connection, take the scissors, athame, or obsidian blade in your dominant hand and say:

   "I sever the ties that connect the energies between [insert name] and myself. I remove all negativity and intentions that no longer serve me. I release you now."

5. Slice through the cords, visualizing your connection ending.

6. Once all the cords have been severed, visualize yourself being surrounded by protective golden light. Say:

   "I am protected from future attachments."

SELF-ACCEPTANCE MIRROR RITUAL

Societal beauty standards make it difficult for many of us to love the skin we are in. Learning to love and accept ourselves is a crucial step toward healing and happiness. This self-acceptance mirror ritual, inspired by Misha Magdalene's ritual in Outside the Charmed Circle, *will set you on the path toward accepting your body as it is. Self-acceptance takes continual work, so perform this ritual often to reaffirm that you are beautiful just the way you are.*

Mirror, large enough to see your full body

1. Completely undress and stand or sit in front of your mirror. This may feel very uncomfortable for you, and that's okay—push yourself to embrace the discomfort.

2. Beginning at your feet and working toward your head, study your body. Run your hands along each part, feeling the perfect imperfections of your skin. If negative self-talk arises, acknowledge them, but don't dwell on them.

3. Spend 5 minutes on each part of your body. Thank it for what it provides you with. For example, thank your feet for providing a foundation and keeping you balanced or thank your abdomen for protecting and supporting you. If something doesn't work as well as you'd like, thank it anyway. You may feel the need to express traumatic emotions. Do so, releasing them into the universe.

4. When you have finished, straighten yourself to your fullest height and say:

   "I am brave, powerful, and accepting of my body."

SHADOW WORK INCENSE

Shadow work is the process of working with our "shadow" or repressed self to gain insights, and ultimately, overcome its negative impacts on our lives. Shadow work is a revealing process that can lead to healing generational trauma, feeling whole, and learning how to meet our needs in a healthy, sustainable way. Getting started on shadow work can be difficult, as it's often easier to ignore a problem than it is to bring it to the surface. If you persevere through the difficulty, shadow work will reward you with the joys of living a happier, healthier life. This incense is designed to help guide and support you during shadow work. It will fill you with healing energy and help you focus, bringing repressed thoughts, emotions, and memories to the surface. Rosemary assists with memory and supports focus, lavender calms and relaxes, lemongrass uplifts, and myrrh helps ground and protect. Burn this incense whenever you wish to engage in any type of shadow work.

1 teaspoon dried rosemary   Mortar and pestle

1 teaspoon dried lavender   Charcoal disk

1 teaspoon dried lemongrass   Fire-safe dish

½ teaspoon myrrh resin   Match or lighter

1. Add herbs to your mortar and pestle and grind into a coarse powder. As you do so, hold your intention firmly in your mind.

2. Add the resin and grind until well distributed, focusing on your intention.

3. When ready to use, light a charcoal disk in a fire-safe dish. When the charcoal is ashy gray, add 1 or 2 teaspoons of loose incense. Store the remainder in an airtight container in a cool, dark place.

PLANTAIN HEALING OIL AND SALVE

Plantain herbs are "weeds" commonly found throughout North America and Eurasia that are magically associated with healing, strength, and protection. This oil or salve can be used to treat minor cuts, insect bites, eczema, and other skin irritations.

FOR THE OIL OR SALVE:

Mason jar with lid

8 rounded tablespoons dried
  plantain leaves

1 cup olive oil

Permanent marker

Slow cooker

Cheesecloth

Brown dropper bottle (for oil) or
  tin container (for salve)

FOR THE SALVE ONLY:

1 ounce beeswax

40 drops lavender essential oil

Double boiler

1. In the mason jar, cover the plantain leaves with the olive oil. Seal.

2. Using a permanent marker, draw an Uruz (healing) or Algiz (protection) (rune) on the lid.

3. Shake the contents while saying the following incantation:

    "Earth's healing gifts are shared with me,
    Through herb and plant and stem and leaf.
    Infuse this oil with your properties,
    So I may partake in your healing energies.
    By my will so it is."

4. Place mason jar in a slow cooker filled with 3 inches of water and cook on low for 6 hours.

5. Strain the contents of the mason jar through a cheesecloth, squeezing to remove excess oil. Compost the remains.

6. If making oil, pour infusion into a brown dropper bottle and store for up to 1 year.

7. If making a salve, pour infused oil and beeswax into a double boiler and heat until beeswax is completely melted. Remove from heat and stir in lavender essential oil. Pour mixture into a tin and store for up to 1 year.

PENDULUM RITUAL TO FIND SPIRITUAL BLOCKAGES

Every witch is on a journey of spiritual growth, which involves learning lessons and breaking patterns. Sometimes, however, we hit a wall and struggle to understand what is keeping us from progressing. Divination is a great way to figure out what is blocking your path. This ritual uses a pendulum to help you find your spiritual blockages and determine what next steps you should take to resolve the issue.

Pendulum

1. Begin by cleansing your pendulum with your preferred cleansing method.

2. Hold the pendulum by the top of the chain between your thumb and index finger.

3. Ask the pendulum to show you *yes* and *no*. These can manifest as any motion. Make note of each answer. Test the pendulum by asking a simple yes-or-no question, such as "Is my name [insert your name]?" If it works, proceed. If not, cleanse and try again.

4. Ask the pendulum, "Do I have a spiritual blockage?"

5. If the answer is *yes*, ask the pendulum to show you where the blockage is on your body by signaling *yes* when it's held over it.

6. Hold the pendulum over each part of your body, starting with your feet and working up to your head.

7. When you have found the blockage, begin asking the pendulum yes or no questions pertaining to potential spiritual blockages associated with that part of your body. For example, if the blockage is your feet, are you running away from something? For more information, you can supplement this ritual with a tarot or rune reading.

8. Follow up by taking mundane actions to remove the blockage, such as facing whatever it is you are running away from.

A Final Word

WHEW! You made it to the end of the book! You are now equipped with a host of magical tips and tricks you can incorporate into your healing and self-care routine. Remember, healing and self-care require constant engagement to work effectively. Self-care is maintenance for your body, mind, and spirit. Just as you routinely change the oil in your car, replace the air filter in your HVAC system, or replace the filters in your water purifier to keep them working as intended, you, too, require maintenance in order to function properly. Prioritizing your needs does not make you selfish or inconsiderate; it's required for you to live your life to the fullest. The more you practice, the better you will get.

Of course, magical self-care is not going to cure everything. Taking a nice, warm bubble bath is not going to fix a toxic work environment, but it can help clear your mind and give you the confidence you need to find a new job. It is important to follow up any magical healing and self-care processes with mundane work. Healing and self-care are an act of liberation and resistance, but only if you are willing to do the work. Remember to fill your cup (self) so that you can fill your cauldron (community).

GLOSSARY

AMULET: a magical object used for protection

ANCESTRAL TRAUMA/ INTERGENERATIONAL TRAUMA: trauma that is inherited by future generations by way of epigenetic changes, due to chronic stress from one's surroundings and environment or surviving a traumatic event such as slavery, famine, pandemic, or war

ASPERGE: a method of cleansing or purification that involves sprinkling a liquid, usually holy water, on a person, place, or thing

ATHAME: a ceremonial blade, usually with a black handle and double edge, used for cutting, carving, and energy directing

CENTERING: the act of pulling your energies into the center of your body before and after spell work

DENDROTHERAPY: the process of energetic healing through communication with trees, usually in the form of touch

DIVINATION: the use of magical or supernatural means to seek knowledge of the future or unknown

EARTHING: a grounding technique that uses direct contact with the earth's surface to transfer energy between you and the earth

GENIUS LOCI: the spirit of place or a tutelary deity of place

GREEN WITCHCRAFT: a secular, earth-based practice that combines the use of natural objects, folk magic, and sustainable, environmentally friendly rituals to honor the earth and nature spirits

GROUNDING: a technique that focuses on realigning energy by reconnecting with the earth; can be done with or without touching the earth itself

INTENTION: a clear and specific desired outcome of a spell, remedy, or ritual

MAGIC(K): the process of manipulating or directing energy to enact desired change

SHADOW WORK: the process of working with your unconscious mind to heal and grow by uncovering repressed or hidden thoughts, emotions, and behaviors

SPELL BAG OR SPELL JAR: a physical representation of a spell inside a bag or jar that can be carried, hung, buried, or stored as needed

TALISMAN: an object imbibed with specific magical powers; usually used to bring luck

ℛESOURCES

Blogs

FLYING THE HEDGE
Visit my blog at FlyingTheHedge.com to learn more about hedgecraft, herbalism, and folklore.

OTHERWORLDLY ORACLE
Visit OtherworldlyOracle.com for a wide range of witchcraft topics, including green witchcraft and spell work.

THE WITCH OF LUPINE HOLLOW
Visit WitchOfLupineHollow.com to learn more about using astrology and witchcraft for self-care.

Books

THE COMPLETE HERBS SOURCEBOOK: AN A-TO-Z GUIDE OF HERBS TO CURE YOUR EVERYDAY AILMENTS BY DAVID HOFFMANN
This book on the medicinal uses of two hundred herbs includes step-by-step guides and preparation instructions.

GREEN WITCHCRAFT: A PRACTICAL GUIDE TO DISCOVERING THE MAGIC OF PLANTS, HERBS, CRYSTALS, AND BEYOND BY PAIGE VANDERBECK
This book is a helpful and informative guide to using green magic.

GRIMOIRE FOR THE GREEN WITCH: A COMPLETE BOOK OF SHADOWS BY ANN MOURA
Learn more about green witchcraft with this comprehensive introduction.

THE MODERN WITCH'S GUIDE TO MAGICKAL SELF-CARE: 36 SUSTAINABLE RITUALS FOR NOURISHING YOUR MIND, BODY, AND INTUITION BY TENAE STEWART

Create rituals to nurture your body, mind, and spirit with this guidebook.

WITCHCRAFT FOR DAILY SELF-CARE: NOURISHING RITUALS AND SPELLS FOR A MORE BALANCED LIFE BY MICHAEL HERKES

Learn about infusing magic into your daily life to create a sustainable self-care practice with this guide.

A WITCH OF THE FOREST'S GUIDE TO NATURAL MAGICK BY LINDSAY SQUIRE

This book is a guide to working green magic in harmony with the environment.

THE WITCH'S BOOK OF SELF-CARE: MAGICAL WAYS TO PAMPER, SOOTHE, AND CARE FOR YOUR BODY AND SPIRIT BY ARIN MURPHY-HISCOCK

This book is a comprehensive introduction to using witchcraft in your self-care practice.

Podcast

EARTH SPEAK BY NATALIE ROSS

This podcast explores working with spirits, connecting with nature, and prioritizing self-care.

REFERENCES

Dawson, S. L., S. R. Dash, and F. N. Jacka. "The Importance of Diet and Gut Health to the Treatment and Prevention of Mental Disorders." *International Review of Neurobiology* 131 (2016): 325–346.

Dias, Brian G., and Kerry J. Ressler. "Parental Olfactory Experience Influences Behavior and Neural Structure in Subsequent Generations." *Nature Neuroscience* 17, no. 1 (2014): 89–96.

"Facts & Statistics." Anxiety & Depression Association of America, September 19, 2021. Accessed May 16, 2022. adaa.org /understanding-anxiety/facts-statistics.

Louv, Richard. *Last Child in the Woods: Saving Our Children from Nature-Deficit Disorder*. Chapel Hill: Algonquin Books, 2008.

Mayo Clinic Staff. "Anxiety Disorders." Mayo Clinic, May 4, 2018. mayoclinic.org/diseases-conditions/anxiety/symptoms-causes /syc-20350961.

Miller, Gretchen M. "4 Trauma-Informed Essentials about the Power of Creative Expression." Starr Commonwealth, January 31, 2020. starr.org/2020/4-trauma-informed-essentials-about-the-power -of-creative-expression.

Piff, Paul K., Pia Dietze, Matthew Feinberg, Daniel M. Stancato, and Dacher Keltner. "Awe, the Small Self, and Prosocial Behavior." *Journal of Personality and Social Psychology* 108, no. 6 (2015): 883. doi.org/10.1037/pspi0000018.

Reis, Harry T., and Susan Sprecher, eds. *Encyclopedia of Human Relationships*. Sage Publications, 2009.

"Self Care for Health." World Health Organization. Regional Office for South-East Asia. (2014). apps.who.int/iris/handle/10665/205887.

Suzman, James. *Work: A History of How We Spend Our Time*. Bloomsbury, 2020.

Yehuda, Rachel, Nikolaos P. Daskalakis, Linda M. Bierer, Heather N. Bader, Torsten Klengel, Florian Holsboer, and Elisabeth B. Binder. "Holocaust Exposure Induced Intergenerational Effects on FKBP5 Methylation." *Biological Psychiatry* 80, no. 5 (2016): 372–380.

Zahn, Roland, Jorge Moll, Mirella Paiva, Griselda Garrido, Frank Krueger, Edward D. Huey, and Jordan Grafman. "The Neural Basis of Human Social Values: Evidence from Functional MRI." *Cerebral Cortex* 19, no. 2 (2009): 276–283.

INDEX

Acknowledgments

I would like to thank my publisher for giving me the opportunity to write another book. This has been such an amazing experience, and I am beyond grateful! Once again, I would like to thank my readers and supporters. Without all of you, there wouldn't be a book. You all are why I do this in the first place. And finally, to my partner and parents, who have never stopped believing in me. I love you dearly.

About the Author

AUTUMN WILLOW is an experienced hedge witch and author of the blog *Flying the Hedge*, where she has been documenting her journey in hedgecraft, spirit communication, and folklore since 2014. With almost twenty years of magical experience, she strives to fill the gap in hedgecraft knowledge, taking a practical approach rooted in science, history, and folklore.

Willow currently resides in Georgia with her three cats and chicken, who enjoy all the snuggles they can get. When she isn't busy casting spells and writing, she enjoys books, movies, and *World of Warcraft*.

CPSIA information can be obtained
at www.ICGtesting.com
Printed in the USA
JSHW011216220223
38046JS00002B/4